D1012933

PEARLS IN VINEGAR

THE PILLOW BOOK OF HEATHER MALLICK

VIKING
CANADA

VIKING CANADA

Published by the Penguin Group

Penguin Group (Canada), 10 Alcorn Avenue, Toronto, Ontario, Canada M4V 3B2
(a division of Pearson Penguin Canada Inc.)

Penguin Group (USA) Inc., 375 Hudson Street, New York, New York 10014, U.S.A.
Penguin Books Ltd, 80 Strand, London WC2R 0RL, England
Penguin Ireland, 25 St Stephen's Green, Dublin 2, Ireland (a division of Penguin Books Ltd)
Penguin Group (Australia), 250 Camberwell Road, Camberwell, Victoria 3124, Australia
(a division of Pearson Australia Group Pty Ltd)
Penguin Books India Pvt Ltd, 11 Community Centre, Panchsheel Park, New Delhi – 110 017, India
Penguin Group (NZ), Cnr Airborne and Rosedale Roads, Albany, Auckland, New Zealand
(a division of Pearson New Zealand Ltd)
Penguin Books (South Africa) (Pty) Ltd, 24 Sturdee Avenue, Rosebank, Johannesburg 2196, South Africa

Penguin Books Ltd, Registered Offices: 80 Strand, London WC2R 0RL, England

First published 2004

1 2 3 4 5 6 7 8 9 10 (RRD)

Manufactured in the U.S.A.

LIBRARY AND ARCHIVES CANADA CATALOGUING IN PUBLICATION

Mallick, Heather
Pearls in vinegar : the pillow book of Heather Mallick / Heather Mallick.

ISBN 0-670-04462-8

I. Title.

PN6331. M24 2004 081 C2004-903546-0

Visit the Penguin Group (Canada) website at **www.penguin.ca**

For Stephen Petherbridge

"Leave us," said Psmith with a wave of his hand.
"We would be alone."
—P.G. Wodehouse

And for my father-in-law,
Harry Petherbridge (1915–1997)

Cleopatra is said to have dissolved a pearl in vinegar and drunk it down, perhaps to prove she could consume a fortune in a single meal, or to give her skin that extra glow, or as an aphrodisiac. Historians disagree as to which daft purpose was hers. The thing is that pearls do not necessarily dissolve in vinegar; not only must they first be crushed but much depends on the acidity of the liquid. These lustrous beads most likely remain intact. The trick for pearls, and for us, is to survive immersion in the "destructive element"—life—of which Joseph Conrad wrote. All our lives are vinegary, even caustic, at times but with care we can keep our pearls opalescent.

—Heather Mallick

"She always had the feeling that it was very, very dangerous to live even one day."

—Virginia Woolf

"Oh come on, Edith, there must be something!"

—Peter Cook on Edith "*Je ne regrette rien*" Piaf

Contents

Introduction

Details, details. Fun as vast generalizations and grand pronouncements are, details are what life is made of and what writers deal in. We observe. On us, nothing should be lost, though most of it is. Don't flatter yourself; your head's just some big old compost heap.

I read *The Pillow Book of Eleanor Bron* years before I had heard of the famous pillow book of Sei Shonagon. The latter was a form of diary, a sheaf of papers made available at the court of the Empress Sadako more than a thousand years ago to a lady-in-waiting named Sei Shonagon. The papers on which she wrote her "occasional writings" were stored inside what we would regard as a most unpillowlike pillow—a curved wooden box on legs. She wrote what she saw and what she thought about what she saw. She was snobbish by our standards—we are trained to conceal our snobbishness—but there is a precision to her observations that appeals to me. She can be harsh, more harsh than I have been permitted to be in this modern pillow book, but I don't have the good fortune to have been dead for a millennium and out of reach of complaints.

Her contemporary Murasaki Shikibu, who wrote *The Tale of Genji,* didn't think much of her—too emotional, she sniffed, too willing to sample each interesting thing that comes along. How can things turn out well for such a woman, she asked. But these are precisely my habits, for good or for ill, I can only say to the tight-lipped Shikibu. Smart people keep their eyes peeled.

A pillow book is not like a diary, which is a sculpted thing, no matter how casual you pretend it is. A pillow book is random and contains just about anything. The wonderful British actress Eleanor Bron, who wrote her pillow book in 1985, subtitling it *An Actress Despairs,* says it's a combination of journal and commonplace book. She calls it "a general sifting of experience," which is a good thing, as I think diaries are attractive to their writers mainly in morose moments. You can't be bothered to write in them when you are having a fantastically good time, so any cheerful bits are only recollected in tranquillity. Much as I savour and collect diaries (yes, I do love reading about other people's miseries), I don't have the ego to think anyone would want to read about my low moments. My attitude to life is Eeyore-ish. So when I vowed to write only about good times, the diaries stopped. But the pillow book continued. Interesting things happen. In fact, I am of the school that everything is interesting, even while painful, and will ring a bell with someone.

Eleanor Bron has the inestimable advantage of her profession. She appeared in things like Beatles movies and was a token woman in the British satirical comedy ensemble Beyond the Fringe. Her pillow book is full of pictures. I will never force you through my photo albums, and as for Sei Shonagon, perhaps there would have been a coffee table book in all her musings had Louis Daguerre got around to starting work on the camera in the year 965.

I'm not dead yet. I don't do pictures. I just do words.

Another word of caution: I am a grown woman. I am deeply troubled by the "girl" fad that began in the 1990s and is continuing in this decade to suck women down a pink rubber drain. One ceases to be a girl at sixteen, yet stumpy, broad-assed, bad-tempered old bags far beyond middle age have started talking and writing as if they were girls. I keep telling these women this is costing them twenty grand in salary; stop giggling and wearing handbags with embroidered cartoons on them.

This doesn't go over well. Funny, they don't seem to care that their words won't be read a thousand years from now, as are those of the sharpish Shonagons. But worse, they're living dull lives that resemble those of so many others; I can't tell these "girls" apart and that's like crumpling someone up and throwing them in the wastepaper basket.

I have a touch of obsessive-compulsiveness and like making lists, and lists of lists. I also like eccentricities and oddities. Jonathan Miller, the polymath British writer and director, is obsessed with fragments. He wrote a book (it would be a coffee table book if the table were very small, is how you'd describe it) called *Nowhere in Particular*. Bet his publishers loved that title—that'll pull the punters in, they would've said sarcastically—but Miller, who is starting to look like an Old Testament god as he ages, would have scythed them or made them cry.

His is also a pillow book with pictures. There are photos of old skips with scraped canvas laced over their tops, fragments of posters left glued to hoardings, rust (he's very keen on rust) and general dereliction. But they're close-ups of decay, not landscapes, and many of them are extraordinarily beautiful.

Miller likes his foveas. The fovea is a tiny area of the retina that can perceive great detail, but this ability falls off suddenly, Miller says, so that if you focus on one word in this text, you can really only see a fog of words around it. Writers of pillow books are using their foveas to see things that they then translate into words. Most people just see the general blur. At times I envy them. Surely they're happier because of it? But it must be dull.

We are living in a time when details matter less and less. A politician kills millions; we are so entranced by the green explosions in the night on TV (in a foreign land, so I'm all right, Jack) that we pass over the minor detail that the war was born of a lie, as most wars are. Much is made of nothing. We follow the Americans in wanting everything bigger, louder, simpler, more garish, more scandalous and always attached to huge sums of money. But the beauty, and the truth, are in the details.

Scientists have been chagrined to discover, via the Human Genome Project, that humans have about thirty thousand genes in their DNA, about the same as your average fruit fly or even weed. "Humans are more like worms than we had ever imagined," an American scientist reported with astonishment. Why astonishment? They had assumed we were terribly complicated. We're not. Arguably this means that Nurture may have had more to say about our characters than Nature.

My nature is Anglo-Indian-Canadian. My father, from Calcutta, was studying architecture and medicine in Glasgow when he met my ultra-Scottish mother who was studying English and philosophy for the purposes of becoming a teacher. They emigrated. His work for the Canadian federal government took him to small towns all over northern Canada where he was doctor of all trades: OB-GYN, pathologist, plastic surgeon and piercer of my teenage ears. My father, a talented surgeon who had no bedside manner but whose stitches were the envy of other doctors, was an enjoyer and occasionally a spender. He loved to hunt and fish; he lived the way he wanted to live, as if he were reborn on this new continent. My mother was a supremely thrifty woman who coped heroically with living in the frozen north and the birth of children (my father delivered us) she may not have wanted. I have never asked. She "tholed," as the Scottish say, enduring suffering without complaint.

What interests me is Nurture. My father was born amid the chaotic hot colours and smells of India. He never spoke of it and never returned. My mother knew the clarity and cleanliness of the Scottish countryside. But really, they were both thrown onto the Siberian white plate of northern Canada, and I was raised in it.

Just as Simon Schama has traced the mark of landscape on nationality, the novelist Margaret Drabble has written extensively about the effect of landscape on personality. Her characters in *The Realms of Gold,* born in the flat, mud-choked Fens, are depressives and suicides. My father was an optimist. My mother was a pessimist, but a strong one. I, raised in the middle of millions of flat hectares of scrub Jack pine and uncountable massive quantities of dry white snow, am a pessimist through and through. And I am convinced that though I inherited my mother's stoicism, I am a depressive by landscape. My worm-sized DNA is half mad and wild, half Calvinist by nature, but oh, it is stark by nurture. Take this into account when you like my observations. I might be wrong, you see. I'm only a nematode, after all.

I hope my pillow book does honour to Sei Shonagon who wrote things like "Anything purple is splendid, be it flowers, thread or paper." I agree. Eleanor Bron mentioned that she was surprised by the heat generated by a mosquito bite that had swollen overnight. She's right about this. I checked.

And now I embark on mine.

1. Men in uniform

Canada held a world festival in 1967 which was called Expo 67 and was such an enormous global success that my parents were happy to take us children to this urban, hip, chic, architectural sex thing in Montreal.

I got lost. I was seven and following a woman in a Mondrian dress when I realized that the woman in the sleeveless cotton dress with black lines enclosing occasional blocks of primary colour was not my mother. Terror choked me. "Where are you from?" said a man leaning down to me. "Ontario," I said helpfully through my sobs.

He took me to an RCMP station within the Expo 67 grounds. They were the Royal Canadian Mounted Police, now much discredited. But they all looked like Fitzwilliam Darcy in *Pride and Prejudice* except they wore scarlet tunics, leather boots to the knee, black leggings and leather belts diagonally across their chests and horizontally on their dented hats. I had only ever seen them in the Musical Ride in which they carried pikestaffs and rode steeds in each other's direction at great speed while music played and onlookers wet themselves.

A Mountie sat me on his lap.

A woman, it has been said, recalls what she was wearing at every significant moment of her life. I was wearing a white pleated miniskirt with a short-sleeved pink top trimmed with white edging and with a large white anchor on the front. He offered me water in a Thermos cup. I shook my head, dazed. The room was strewn with long carelessly angled male legs and leather boots, packed with men's voices and cigarette smoke. I was high on maleness, dazed by it, but was not yet at the age to understand what I was seeing or to have explicit sexual feelings.

My parents came to rescue me. I regretted this.

Every kindness, every surge of desire I have shown to men in my life, was born in this moment.

Decades later, on my first morning in Paris, I am fresh off the plane and sitting dazedly in the Café Sully waiting for my hotel room to become available. I am wearing a comfortable travel dress, a black cotton version of a Diane von Furstenberg with a very long skirt and a V that reveals a lot of breast if I'm not careful. I am eating blood sausage with greedy pleasure. Then a troop of men in Napoleonic uniforms canter by on huge white horses, short fat soldiers who look like Beatrix Potter's Jeremy Fisher in their tight white pants, scarlet tunics thick with gold braid and magnificent cakelike hats, all in perfect formation. I watch in astonishment and admiration. I gape, I'll give them that. I then realize that every man on horseback is eyes right, staring at my tits.

2. Snake balls are shocking things

Snake balls are shocking things, especially in retrospect. I was very young and not afraid of the garter snakes we occasionally saw slipping through the grass on the hill on which our house was placed.

One day, wandering though the woods, deep inside the trees but not too far from my swing set, I came across a large writhing ball of snakes, all yellow-white, as, for some reason, their bellies were turned outside, perhaps for some sexual signalling reason. The garter snakes were diving into the ball, stroking, sliding and mating presumably, but with such precision that the ball was perfectly round. Snakes that escaped the ball would be right side up on the woodland floor, greenish-brown, but would again enter the tightness of the ball by some means.

I stared. I did not run. I simply registered.

To this day, I loathe snakes. I read Margaret Atwood's snake poems and try to see them as she does, as raw bracelets, slack ropes, thin lines. She, snarky snake fancier, suggests gasoline and a match for snake balls. I'll always wriggle with disgust at snakes. Yet I used to send money to the Jersey Trust, an animal preservation organization, whenever the late Gerald Durrell was seeking to expand his snake house. I was paying alimony, stay-away money, to snake balls the way you donate money to Aversion Therapy for Pedophiles, anything to get them off the front step.

3. Name what plagues you

Name what plagues you after people who plague you. It's great fun and you kill two birds with one stone.

Hoons: The dark circles under my eyes caused by sleeplessness/misery/heredity are named after Geoff Hoon, British Prime Minister Tony Blair's minister of defence, who helped drive Dr. David Kelly to suicide in 2003 after the doctor secretly briefed a BBC reporter on the government's invented claim that Iraqis had "weapons of mass destruction." Hoon has the coarse features and thick wet lips of a heavy, a wide boy, a "lout" as indeed is the OED definition of a hoon. Imagine sex with a hoon. A woman can't sink lower than that.

Gardena: Much less beautiful than a gardenia, this is the blackish bump on my right arm that, to go by my history of scar healing, will be with me for another six years. When you're trimming tree branches with a Gardena lopper and it won't quite cut through the wood, don't leave the lopper and branch suspended while you tug smartly on the cord. The entire mess will land on you, cutting your arm and causing extreme pain that you will manfully conceal from watching neighbours until you can get in the house and sob. Its proper name is Gardena; its descriptive name is Garden Folly.

GardenaMort: The Gardena secateurs that my husband, Stephen, henceforth to be known as S., used to briskly amputate his fingertip as he was pruning while fretting about one of the teenagers. Gardena prides itself on making the best garden tools. True, they cut through limbs like butter. But I paid them back. Those secateurs lie in pieces with old diapers and raccoon corpses in a distant dump. Bet that GardenaMort's sorry now.

Zurichs: I use Yves Saint Laurent's Touche Éclat to conceal my Hoons. But I also use them to cover up the reddish area where the nostrils meet the face. I have named these reddish C's my Zurichs, after my car insurer, who dumped me into the lap of ING, a grabby little Dutch firm that forces me to insure my children for driving their father's lovely expensive pristine car which, trust me, he will never let them do after seeing what they did to the perfect yet unglamorous car we bought them. Every morning, I am to be found ZurichING my red zones and cursing them anew.

Poindexter: A wedgie caused by thong underwear is a Poindexter, Ronald Reagan's Nicaraguan Contras man who popped up again in 2002 wanting to put all Americans under electronic surveillance and who dreamed up a 2003 Pentagon online scheme where citizens would bet on when the next act of terrorism would hit the U.S. Since everyone knows the house always wins, the criminal possibilities of the government running a terrorism casino made even the Republicans nervous. He got nowhere except up everyone's ass. Also known as "Elliot Abrams," with his slits for eyes and pointy slit of a face. They slide in. Poindexters are endemic to little girls, who are distressed until you tell them that their glamorous older cousins live with them, too. This calms them. Coping with Poindexters is all about growing up.

Cultural Revolution: My mother's arthritis, which surrounds her with jabbering Red Guards with eyes full of hate and invades her with pain while she maintains her dignity and determination.

Jillys: Foolish remarks, the memory of which used to keep me awake with 4:48 Psychosis, until I realized that a Jilly here, a Jilly there won't matter. I will make many more Jillys in my life. Named after Jilly Cooper, the doggy, gap-toothed, silly British author who is always going on about sex being a jilly jolly romp but who doesn't seem to mind making Jillies, so I suppose I don't either. Just so I can get back to sleep.

Fredwards: Men who are attracted to you but fear your rejection and therefore dislike you, no, resent you with a poison they'd clearly like to dip their arrow into and drop you with a blow dart. My first Fredward was a little boy in Grade 3 who gathered his little friends to pin me up against a fence on my way home for lunch and kissed me against my will. I hated him. Keep a weather eye out for Fredwards.

Shigellas: They're dirty women. They may be kind, though this is unlikely, and well-dressed, although this won't last. What they are is dirty. Their nostrils are unkempt, their roots undyed and hair unwashed. Often their clothes are expensive but always look as though they've been slept in. Those who don't know the meaning of *shigella* may call them "Ms. Dirty Bra Straps." I once borrowed a stroller from a Shigella for a visiting infant relative. It looked as though it had lived through a mudslide, and when disassembled for transport it leaked black goop (Satan's spackle) from its metal joints onto the car upholstery. I winced; my S. had a fit. Apparently, men, who have the reputation of being careless of their hygiene, have a horror of Shigellas. This raises men in my estimation. Bernie Taupin was for a time notorious for the misogynist lyrics on Elton John's *Goodbye Yellow Brick Road.* But I do now see the point of saying "Alice, I bet she hasn't had a bath in years." Not that Taupin wasn't a Fredward; he clearly was.

Scabia Gloriosus: One thing rarely made clear to the children of wealthy people is that the money's spent mostly for show; there isn't much left for the offspring to fling around. And so they swan about with their pretensions and their dreams of mansions, thinking they're gloriosus but by the economic = moral standards they were raised with, they're really just Scabia being munched by slugs. And it isn't the silly things they say, it's the clenched-jaw "Massachusetts malocclusion" with which they scrape their words out. I remember going to a Scabia Gloriosus party once, where the hostess said to us, "Here's the most valuable thing in my house." She showed us an antique doll. The corner of her dining room was filled with African totems, i.e., gravestones, which she had bought to sell at vast prices to Dodgy Brother Antiques, never mind the poor sod who had been counting on the totem to achieve something in the afterlife. She was the sort of woman who had paid top price for silent toilets, the kind that are so silent they don't actually flush properly. You cross your fingers and flush repeatedly, which rather defeats the purpose of pretending that toilets are not necessary to Gloriosus types. We've all met them. *Sic transit* the scabs on their (imaginary) glories.

Subcutanei: These are things that stay with you, floating at the bottom of the brain pond. For instance, in a Pink Panther movie,

Inspector Dreyfuss, driven mad by Clouseau, his nose shot off and his twitch and insane laugh back in commission, calls Clouseau:

Clouseau: *"Who is this?"*

Dreyfuss: *"Can't you guess? It's the man who hates you, who wants to see you dead and buried in your grave!"*

Clouseau: *(suspiciously) "Are you the headwaiter at that little bistro on the rue Tragords?"*

Noodling: Bad jazz is "noodling." Noodling on the piano, the sax, whatever. Philip Larkin was right: When jazz ceased to resemble the sound of the human voice, it changed into something dead. Modern jazz, alien to the human heart, is not music. It demands no talent; it's like the soundtrack of a hot, small-town afternoon when you're fourteen and powerless and the only point of time is that it's passing, never fast enough for a fourteen-year-old who wants out of that small town.

Plinking: Piano that accompanies crooners. "Plink plink." It's the humiliation of a fine instrument.

4. Things that make you appreciate men

The elevator stops. It just stops. There are four of us. We wait. We wait. It will never move. Claustrophobic, I crouch down in the back corner and start making a moaning sound. A man, a complete stranger, puts his hand gently on my shoulder to comfort me. I am becalmed. The elevator restarts and we all depart. This was twenty years ago and I still wish I had told him how rare he was and said thank you. Another failure on my part, I see.

When I am flattened by depression, S. quotes Samuel Beckett at me. "I can't go on … I'll go on." The puzzling thing is that it works.

I dislike wearing bras and panties that don't match. It offends my sense of symmetry. Nevertheless, my underwear never matches, unless I know S. is going to see it, in which case I wear expensive, matching things in pinks and mauves and beige satin. This is one way that men buff you up and improve you, at times when you just cannot be arsed to do it.

Before pornographic spam become common, it must have been awful for guys in the office. Why were they getting all that mail about their small penises, personally directed at them? Who snitched? Was it that woman they met on the train that time? Look, a train toilet isn't ideal for sex. Cold, didn't smell nice. They can do better, they must have reassured themselves. My girlfriend has actually slept with a man who had a huge one. It was awful, she said with indignation. It hurt. What, am I having a baby here, she was thinking resentfully. Never yearn for what you are told to yearn for. It will be a giant con.

5. Men I never slept with

A security guard at the Paris department store BHV who stopped me when I entered the store and after some detective work to which I did not object, discovered that the thongs I'd bought for my stepdaughter (I myself do not wear a cheese wire in my crotch though he was not to know this) at Monoprix still had their security tag. He then asked me for something the next night that presumably involved removing the cheese wire, at which point I wanted to say I was not only married (this was not relevant, I see now) but leaving the country on Sunday. But I was so horrified that all my French left me including the word for Sunday. We are going to Sainte-Chapelle, I told him (a medieval cathedral on the Ile de la Cité). If there is a more idiotic reason not to sleep with a security guard who looks like a rat with glasses and has the power to interrogate you in a small French cell in the tool-ridden hardware floor of a giant department store, a claim to a previously booked viewing of some fabulous stained glass is hard to beat.

A man who told me that a) I was too exotic-looking to be named Heather and was more of a Eugenie or some peculiar thing, b) his damning evaluation of my summer as an intern could easily be rewritten and c) I would have to fuck him to get hired. I wish I had done a Naomi Wolf and vomited, but instead I left the building and still shiver as I pass it. On the other hand, when you live in a city for twenty-five years, half the real estate inspires post-traumatic stress.

A colleague who landed on me in the back of a cab like something expelled from a great height by a seagull and began kissing me wetly and heavily. I was appalled but said nothing and moved not. Eventually he hauled himself off and mumbled an apology.

A date, a nice dark-haired young man, whose apartment I was visiting for the first time. His bathroom floor had never been swept. It was covered with fine dark hair. I stared. I gagged. I left. As you get older, hygiene becomes not a repellent word referring to sex ed classes but a desirable, indeed essential, quality in a male.

One year, when I realized the cash was flowing and would continue to do so, I decided to embark on electrolysis, never having to shave my legs in the shower being a distant dream of mine. How distant I only discovered later—it takes years of appointments with the space between each gradually lengthening—and it's addictive. My electrologist Christabel warned me about that. Eventually, you'd start doing your head if you could, she said. She was a kind woman, and I came to know her fairly well as each session could last an hour or perhaps two. We'd chat. She was big, heavily made-up, had a fairly empty love life, was a rollerblader etc. She had very hairy arms, I noticed. She and her colleagues used to "do" each other when they had time.

Being flush, I eventually got around to buying an ounce of dope. I got very high one night and passed out in bed. And just as I was sliding into unconsciousness, I sat up straight. "My God," I said.

"Christabel's a man!" And of course she was. Talk about opening the doors of perception. Chris(tabel) had never said anything about it. She must have been unsure just how clueless I was. I now realize she was dropping hints like dumbbells on my toes.

6. Female infidelity

Female infidelity, once thought so rare, is running rampant, a friend tells me. She knows almost no women who are faithful to their husbands. But most married men are unfaithful. Are they only unfaithful with single women? It seems unlikely, since such affairs rarely go well. All this time, we haven't been wondering about the huge gap between the number of men having sex and the number of women. Who on earth are they sleeping with?

A book once scared the hell out of me, offering lurid stories of married women who had office affairs with married men. The problem seemed to be that the women invariably fell in love with the men, while the men were empty vessels without feeling. Thus the women suffered years of anguish, poisoned their own marriages and made work a combination of sexual arousal and emotional wounding, while the guy was worried sick about his missing stapler or something.

Maybe it isn't sexual passion that drives these affairs. It's either availability or the fact that something must be done to make work interesting. The dullness of almost all employment is beyond words, which is why movies, novels, sitcoms etc. never show people doing actual work. Imagine having a reason not to wear your comfy underwear to work but to wear something minimal to match your shaved crotch and your dancing mind that gets you so moist you end up with a scalding yeast infection (which, now that I think about it, is a highly believable reason not to hump the newly duller husband). It gives you a reason to live. Later, it gives you a reason to die of unhappiness. Or self-loathing. What have you got yourself into?

I read a short story once in which a man announced to his wife and children on speaker phone that he was leaving them for another woman. It's better than a fax, but still. I call it a Becker, after Boris Becker who admitted he impregnated a total stranger in the broom closet of a bar while his wife was in hospital with labour pains. The only thing worse would have been a broom closet in the hospital. Perhaps he was lying. Do bars have broom closets? Hospitals certainly do. I suppose the child is called Moppet.

7. Et cetera

I dislike technical words for sex, perhaps because my father was an OB-GYN. I say "cunt" all the time, often as a term of amused abuse. I know I shouldn't but to me it's such a casual, funny word. But if a man used it, I'd be enraged, most unfairly. I cannot make myself say "penis" out loud. So I just call it "willy" or "thing." I don't want to use slang like "bangers and mash" that I think demeans men. To avoid using the disgusting word "balls," I say "goolies." But on they go using that awful word "pussy" which is so Hugh Hefner in 1962, so Rat Pack, so dead and gone.

And it's ironic because the thing I like most about men is the vulnerability of their genitals. There they hang, the goolies and the shy willy, borne about by every single man I meet and I almost have to stop myself laughing at the pity of it. It's soft. It's totally outside you! Aren't you worried it'll get hurt? Or cold? Poor sweet.

Unless he's violent or loathsome for some other reason, I find it difficult to dislike a naked man. I feel such fondness for him, such affection. Take care, I want to say. Mind how you go. Don't climb any fences. Ouch.

I have never understood how a man could strike a woman. But they do. They look at her naked, her breasts so vulnerable, and they regularly rip women to shreds. I look at what could hurt me and feel affection; a man looks at softness and feels the ability to hurt what is hurtable.

I will never understand this. And I will never understand why I, a feminist, should like men so very much and feel sorry for their predicament.

8. People who stolidly fall

People who stolidly fall into their parents' line of work are often sullen and talentless. Nepotism is a soft bed but the nails are underneath. My father once complained of a right hand so badly bruised that he had difficulty answering the phone. He had been out the previous night delivering a baby. If that was the hand, imagine the birth canal. I immediately resolved not only not to deliver babies for a living, but never to be in the position of having to expel one.

Talent skips generations anyway. The plodding carbon copy child will spend her career cursing her cowardice. This does not apply to skilled people, of course. An instinct for plumbing or laying a glossy, squeakless birch floor can easily be passed on to a willing child. An accountant whose child can't add should be out celebrating. Imagine the joy of having a good plumber in the family. Oh, the pride of it!

9. Things I have never done

Ridden a bike

Swum (can't, don't)

Read a newspaper editorial (won't)

Successfully killed a leech, whether by burning cigarette, salt or beating it to death and throwing in actual fire

Caught the ball

Drawn blood

Eaten snake

Visited any Eastern European nation

Seen *It's a Wonderful Life*

Seen *Thelma and Louise*

Yelled at my mother

Been yelled at by my mother

Been pregnant

10. My husband's wordplay

Why can't I find the cheap dental floss, I say with annoyance, searching the kitchen drawers. We use so much and it always breaks. "Ah," says S., "you're worried about the bill on the floss."

My next-door neighbour and my husband both mow their front and back lawns. S. is delighted. They have cut a "four-lawn figure," or a "fore-lorn" figure, as S. says in his English accent, with great satisfaction.

My husband and I get on an elevator. It is made by the Schindler company, a small plaque announces. "Schindler's Lift," says S.

I meet a girlfriend for lunch. "Whatja have?" S. asks, this being a family joke extracted from a British TV comedy called *The Royle Family* that we watch like demons. "A caprese salad and some kind of veal thing." "Yes, women eat a caprese salad with their meat," he says dreamily. Yeats wrote "It's certain that fine women eat a crazy salad with their meat." And S.'s pun moment has arrived.

11. Overheard

A group of people is arguing on the sidewalk, trying to decide on a restaurant. One snaps, "Okay, you tell me your definition of *normal* food."

"I've seen Starlight Express. On *Ice*."

"We were only in Paris for two days. So we ate Thai. Didn't want to risk anything."

Oldster conversation:

Geezer 1: *"Who directed* Dirty Rotten Scoundrels*?"*

Geezer 2: *"Who directed it? I'll look it up." He hauls out Leonard Maltin's film guide.*

Geezer 1: *"Who wrote that?"*

Geezer 2: (distractedly) "Leonard Maltin."

Geezer 1: "Leonard Maltin directed Dirty Rotten Scoundrels? *I never knew that."*

And so on for hours, these two old guys. I come home, worried that my job is aging me prematurely and that my arteries are hard as bullwhips.

12. Elegant things

Toile de jouy. Why printed fabric with young French boys playing outside a rustic woodman's cottage should be elegant eludes me, but it does the trick.

Fortuny scarves sold in a small shop called Venetia Studium in Venice. An Aladdin's cave of crumpled silks in colours you've never seen before: the blue at the heart of an iceberg, the green when you spit on a dark leaf, the rust that is the colour of old, old blood.

Alabaster

Marzipan

Laguiole cheese knives, with blue handles, gold rivets and a steel bee where the curved blade begins

The breasts of Lesley-Anne Down. This British actress has the most beautiful breasts in existence, like small, perfectly shaped apples. I've seen them twice, once in a film called *Hanover Street,* which was an attempt to remake a World War II tearjerker, and again in a British TV cop show called *The Sweeney*. She's a stunning woman still. I wonder if those breasts have changed over the years. Sometimes I look at clothes and think, "Only a woman with the breasts of Lesley-Anne Down could wear that garment."

13. Things sold in BHV

Bazar de l'Hotel de Ville is a Paris department store that is best described as a gay Canadian Tire. At home, I go to unglamorous stores like Canadian Tire and Carpet World and get out fast, mainly because S. is deeply bored by shopping of any kind. It seems to make him almost angry, but I shudder to think how greasily and uncomfortably we would live if I weren't willing to irritate him by shopping. But especially in the basement hardware section of BHV, I go into a trance of accumulation. Eventually I have to reconsider items that I chose not because I needed them but because I was dazed by the revelation that they were sold there. One must be practical.

The store guide handed out to shoppers is artistic but most peculiar, printed in an oddly translated English. It lists, among many other things, Adhesive, Armchairs, Backpack, Beauty appliances,

Cellar items, Clothes-horse, Cork floor and wall, Doormats, Garden's structures and ornaments, Glues, Haberdashery, Knobs & Pegs & Handles, Lingerie, Men's underwears, Moulding, Passementerie, Petshops, Rope, Scales, Stockings & Tights, Table linen, Taps, Ties, Tiles, Umbrellas, Watering, Women's underwears and Wood floor. It would seem as though many things are missing, but I always home in on my target at BHV and wander lost through North American department stores.

Among the things I eventually buy are tiny gold padlocks to wear as jewellery (as I am feeling particularly femalely oppressed lately and this is symbolic, not that anyone ever catches the lock-and-key reference); blue bathroom tiles shaped like long pencils for edging the table for my twin bathroom sinks; little see-through purple plastic boxes to store cosmetics; and three small corn-coloured Yves Delorme towels that are the perfect size for use as hair towels, a matter of measuring that is beyond the ken of the rest of the world's towel makers, apparently.

And then I go to the only washroom in the store, which is on the fifth floor and unisex. You'd think the world's best hardware store, with its terrific plumbing department, could pull off a brilliant toilet that would please both flavours. Non. It is filthy and no one can look anyone else in the eye. On the escalator, I clean my hands with a Handi Wipe.

And while we're at it, the main floor women's washroom at Harrods, which charges a pound a pee, is so homely one is embarrassed for them. We should charge them.

14. Building a good bed

Building a good bed isn't easy for people who don't need beds or don't spend much time in them, anyone under twenty, say. I suppose they do their rutting on the kitchen table. But sensualists need them. They should be as huge as the staircase that allows their delivery, even if you have to patch the wall a bit afterwards. No matter how expensive the mattress, it should have a featherbed (a goosedown padding) covered by an extra-deep mattress pad to hold everything in place. You need thick cotton sheets (buy the topsheet a size larger as it will shrink in the wash) and blankets that reflect your nature. Some people like a heavy weight of coverlets on their bodies while others feel smothered and have duvets. Everyone with a duvet is wrong. It's that simple. How do they even know they're in bed? No, you need a lead blanket, which is cozy (and protects you from nuclear attack). And then you need a bedspread that is soft for naps. A foam pillow is always best—it gives and bounces back—but they are almost impossible to find now, perhaps because the polyesterists were so busy showing off.

What you're aiming for is a padded cell built horizontally. As for sleep, I think humans need nine hours minimum. Few of us achieve it, but we must all try. Oh, the pleasures of indolence.

15. Poetic subjects

Anything with sand on it

Anything Martin Parr, the Pieter Bruegel the Elder of everyday life, decides to photograph. He's the man who came up with a book called *Boring Postcards*. He takes photos of gooseberry-growing contests in English villages and publishes entire books of couples sitting silently in restaurants avoiding each other's eyes.

Rubbishy old wooden screen doors that slam (thanks, Bruce Springsteen)

Women looking worried

Objects that are empty, like shoes

Detritus on a plate

Old cosmetics, dried up over the years

16. My first memory

My first memory is of being in my crib, wailing because everyone was elsewhere and I was left alone behind chipped metal bars. Everything was white. There was a jar of Nivea in my crib, on its side in the corner. Is this why I love blue and am obsessed with creams and lotions? Was it the sight of an orange silk throw with a golden fringe in my grandfather's house in Scotland that made me crave colour all my life despite being born in a colourless house in a white and faded green northern landscape? I was very angry. I believe my mother came in eventually.

17. Possible responses to trauma

The most widely disseminated way, popularized by Americans, is to talk about it.

The most practical way, as espoused by British soldiers post-1945, is to never mention it again.

Make a joke of it. I do this.

Build an invisible electric fence around it and place all Rottweiler thoughts, Caliban encounters and Bundy/Shipman memories in this pen. A brick wall is better but harder to mentally electrify. It's not a question of mentioning, but of thinking. No Thinking Past This Wall. It works marvellously well.

Pretend it happened to someone else. This is a technique notoriously favoured by abused children. They divide themselves into two and the other one suffered. It causes terrible problems in later life but it gets you through kidhood which is all any kid ever asked.

18. Things that take one aback

A total stranger approaches in a store. "Your purse is dripping," she says. It was only Evian, not bile or blood from a can, but no less of a shock to be told.

I am maniacally tidy, almost to the extent of obsessive-compulsion. When I visit my sister, I automatically remove everything from her fridge and scrub it all down. My nieces are told that Auntie Heather will be visiting next month. "Ooh," says Sarah, "the aunt who comes to clean." Both girls begin removing jam jars from the fridge.

In Margaret Atwood's *The Robber Bride,* two sophisticated teenage girls refer to "cunt gum." It is the first time I have heard any human refer to this substance. It is cunt wetness that gets a bit solid and is not unpleasant in yourself or a loved one. Yet you are astounded to hear it from Atwood of all people.

My little niece is hugging me. I feel her hand patting me on the back, as if I have suffered some loss and need consolation. It occurs to me that her mother pats her on the back to calm her. She has noticed this and is simply reproducing it for the adult holding her. It's a strangely elderly gesture for a freshly minted person.

The pillows at the Hotel Arts in Barcelona are the finest pillows on which I have ever laid my worried head. I call Housekeeping and ask if I can buy one to take home. She says no. So many people steal the pillows that they have none to spare. I wonder. Am I being invited to steal it? I don't, of course.

An obese American woman walking along the rue de Rivoli in Paris at 8 A.M. eating a hamburger.

I am reading Jean Shepherd's *In God We Trust: All Others Pay Cash*. He's the man who inspired that great eccentric film *A Christmas Story*. This is a collection of his pieces from the 1960s, many of which were published in *Playboy*. It's all fairly pleasant, like his humour. Then I come across this passage: "Lolita has no Male counterpart. A male kid is really a kid. A female kid is a girl. Some guys give up early in life, surrender completely before the impassable transparent wall, and remain little kids forever. They are called 'Fags.'"

At this point, I go off Shepherd. A lot of gay young men must have killed themselves in days when men like Shepherd ran the world.

The Clinton White House aide Sidney Blumenthal has written a memoir. I always had sympathy for the man, who was snitched on during the Ken Starr madness, and falsely, by someone he called a friend. In another case of betrayal, Blumenthal writes with shock and pain at being called "a human ferret" by right-wing columnist Michael Kelly. Kelly had two faces, one kindly and one Ripper-ish. Just as Blumenthal's book was published, Kelly died horribly in Iraq where he had rushed off to cover the war. The Humvee in which he was travelling with U.S. soldiers overturned into a ditch. I assume the dead had the usual crushed torsos, snapped backs and severed parts wetted by a blood fountain that are never described in news reports of car accidents. Few of us are granted the kind of revenge handed to Blumenthal. Cannot help thinking that his feelings must have been mixed. I envy him. It's as if a Monty Python god had thundered "Human ferret, eh?" and crushed Kelly with his giant finger. The same goes for the death by cancer of Robert Bartley of *The Wall Street Journal*'s editorial pages, who drove Vince Foster to suicide. Foster said Washington was a place where "ruining people is considered sport." Bartley was a true sportsman.

The hurt look on the face of a Paris waiter when he sees that you have not managed to consume all of the delicately flavoured but massive flatfish that covered your plate. I am recovering from a malady, I explain, hoping my French can convey worlds of illness, and that my presence in the restaurant was out of kindness to my food-deprived husband. But you know the waiter is thinking "Could do better," like a school report card.

Coming home from a trip to Hong Kong to find S.'s divorce decree in the mail.

In another envelope is a lawsuit from a car dealership from which we leased a car. We have an attack of gentility: We are not the Sued Type! When S. calls them, annoyed, they admit they sent it out automatically. No one has *ever* made their final lump sum payment on a lease without being sued, they say.

19. Things that take one aback on second thought years later

Earl Spencer's eulogy for Princess Diana was roundly admired, is even now being used as a text on rhetoric in British schools. Now one discovers that he rarely saw her, taunted her with her "mental illness," forced her to return the family tiara thirteen years after he gave it to her so his own wife would have it (the wife he cheated on soon after his wedding, the same wife he would later divorce) and ultimately took possession of her wedding dress to display at his family home despite her stated wish that it go to the Victoria & Albert Museum. My record of bastard-spotting has once again gone splat.

20. Things that take one aback without any thought whatsoever

I go out to dinner at Le Train Bleu above the Gare de Lyon, where in a gilded room coated with paintings of cherubs and courtiers I drink champagne and such a great deal of wine that the praise I lavish on the waiter who removes the head, fins and spine of my sole is over the top, no matter how good the guy is. On the way home, I lean on S.'s arm and sing fragments of "These Foolish Things" very loudly indeed. "An airline ticket that bears a lipstick's traces, wild somethings only seven francs a kilo," I bellow happily.

Back in our apartment rented from a trusting man named Grant, I attempt to hang my raincoat on a rack of coat hooks which does not appear to exist. I coulda sworn there was a huge pile of coat hooks on this wall, I mumble. After several attempts to hang my coat on a smooth wall devoid of anything resembling a hook, I say what the hell, pull my clothes off and pass out in fine humour, still singing bits of things. The next morning I wake up and realize that the entire twenty-kilo coat rack had fallen off the wall while we were out and is now resting comfortably on the floor which was the last place a drunk would think to look.

I swear, Grant, the thing just fell off. We didn't do it. It just happened. But he's going to believe that?

So we have the bedspread dry-cleaned just to be polite (in a hotel, I always avoid lying on the bedspread as god knows who's done what on it) because we don't know how to fix the coat rack. We then encounter the French attitude to retail: The Customer Is Always Wrong. The woman at the dry cleaners says it doesn't look dirty to her. We are no more able to explain to her that "we just feel like cleaning it" than we are to Grant that "it fell off on its own, I swear." When I get home, I send the guy flowers and give up on explaining.

An American reader of a column opposing the American war in Iraq writes to me that I deserve to be "ass-fucked by an AIDS-infected nigger." Go round smugly telling everyone what cave-dwelling Yank in Alabama has said. But later, as the thought swirls, I realize that only one element in his vile wish actually repels—the AIDS bit. Otherwise, it sounds interesting rather than offensive.

The Independent writes of the furor that has followed an American scientist's study suggesting there is indeed a cure for homosexuality. It turns out to be bollocks, apparently based on talk therapy provided by Christian fundamentalists treating gays who were experiencing little gaiety. But it did appear that two hundred people no longer thought the same way about their own sex—they avoided temptation, suppressed erotic thoughts and mixed socially with straights in non-sexual situations.

I translate this as going on holiday in Albania, undergoing electric shocks when shown pictures of hot, sexy gays and taking welding courses with the kind of people who are keen to do their own ironmongering rather than hiring someone. The serial killer and child-chopper Frederick West did a lot of his own ironwork.

But it occurred to me that the proof would be in the pudding if scientists managed to "cure" me of my heterosexuality. Sure, I'll be their guinea pig because as long as I get sex with what I want, I don't mind what I want, if you follow me.

Presumably the definition of a heterosexual situation is a man and a woman being alone together. Since I am married, S. and I are frequently alone together but only mad people would regard even 50 percent of that time as sexual. Before we got married, we would meet specifically to have sex. Admittedly, we combined this with other activities like drinking wine, having music on in the background and noticing later that our knees were bleeding.

But when you're married you can't do this all day. Most situations—making dinner, swabbing whitener on the bathtub grouting and arguing over whether the cherry tree is dead or just resting for a season—are non-sexual.

At this point, let's dismiss the third thing, mixing socially with straights in non-sexual situations. The time I spend with other men in non-sexual situations is even less erotic than this. Having told a policeman that my garden shed has been broken into and my lawnmower stolen (and explaining why he should care, frankly) and a Parisian doctor at 2 A.M. that when I vomited blood after eating a rank patisserie it was more of a splotch event than an actual spurting (at which point he lost interest), I now realize that I am never in sexual situations with men. Yes, a man in uniform at De Gaulle Airport asked if he could see my "yeux jolies," but given that he was in Passport Control and I was wearing huge dark sunglasses, he was hardly making a pass.

Thus the only way to make a lesbian out of me is to attach jellied pads to my limbs and torso and apply electric shocks while being shown pictures of attractive men.

This is funny because when women see attractive men, their bodies already respond with electric shocks. These dodgy doctors may not be aware of the female sexual response. We women get little "sensations" in our lower abdomen that make us jump or at least shift uneasily in our chairs. Our eyes widen, we blink repeatedly and sometimes the feeling is so intense that I wrap my legs around themselves so that my left foot goes in front of my right leg, pokes around the back and reappears at the front, anything to stop the twitching. S. can do this to me regularly.

This happens at times that would not strike a man as sexual. I will be watching an episode of *Inspector Morse* for instance and Morse snaps, "I hate men who beat up women." What a guy. S. points out with his usual tact that not only is Inspector Morse an imaginary character but the great actor John Thaw passed away two years ago. I am thus drawn to a man who does not exist on at least two levels, a double simulacra. The joke is definitely on me.

The attraction of men's fine minds sparks something, although it may not be shocks exactly. I had a wonderful lunch once with British writer John Mortimer, but he was seventy-three years old at the time and frighteningly fat. We had drunk two bottles of a really potent Valpolicella and I was so drunk after the lunch I took a wrong turn outside the restaurant and wandered about the green downtown campus of my old university mumbling to myself, "This place looks familiar." (I spent five years studying there.) Those

American gays trying to switch back should remember never to drink heavily. Anything could happen.

But I am not normal. I don't know who Johnny Depp is. I've never seen his face, couldn't ID him in a police lineup. But most women apparently quiver like peeled Hydro cables when they see him in a movie. Given the choice between meeting Johnny Depp while being shocked with a cattle prod and not being shocked with a cattle prod at all, most women would choose Johnny Depp and prod.

Aversion therapy does not work on us. We like whom we like. This explains abusive marriages. I can't speak for homosexuals, of course. I'm just saying that this therapy would be worse than useless in my case, as my taste is inexplicable. Dudley Moore, for instance—tiny but lovely.

21. Speaking of Dudley Moore

Speaking of Dudley Moore, I read in a biography that he thought the following story was hilarious, and it was. A friend's mother had seen a stage production of *The Sound of Music* in which the Mother Superior was played by a woman with a heavy German accent. And in that scene when Maria pours out her troubles to her, the Mother asks her "What *is* it you can't face?" which, in a German accent, came out as "Vat is it you cuntface?" I don't know what this says about me that I think this is the funniest thing I've ever heard, but what does it say about S. that several times, in the depths of despair,

I have read a letter or taken a phone call and, utterly shattered, said "Oh my god, I can't face it." And S., no matter how bad the news is, is always there to say innocently, "What is it, you cuntface?" I'm sorry but this cracks me up every time. They should put it on my tombstone. I'd love to have an epitaph where no one gets the joke. It would be the story of my life.

22. Nipples and willies, etc.

A British parliamentary sketchwriter I admire once did a wrong and unkind thing. He reported on a female MP standing up to address a question to the prime minister and said her nipples were hard as she spoke. He said straight out that power must indeed be an aphrodisiac.

If there were ever proof that women can't win, it's this. For women's nipples harden for any number of reasons: cold, at random, arousal, tension. I have no explanation for why one of them hardens for no reason and the other doesn't. But there's no reason to offer hard nipples as evidence that the ragged-toothed Tony Bliar, as he is now widely known, aroused the woman MP. If the sketchwriter had asked any woman he'd ever slept with, he'd know that. And it was some boring question about traffic roundabouts or something.

But since he was crude and stupid enough to write it, I feel able to ask a question about the six white men in suits who surrounded a smiling President George W. Bush in November of 2003 as he signed a bill banning women from having late-term abortions. The bill would likely cause the deaths of some pregnant women, definitely endanger the lives of some and will result in the kind of births that aren't ever discussed: babies with no brains, eyeless blobs etc.

All the men clapped as they surrounded their commander-in-chief seated at his desk. They were backed by a wall of flags. What I want to know is, how many of those men's organs were erect? Your dominion over women's genitals is being proclaimed by your commander-in-chief; you're on film; you're part of a small group chosen to surround the president as he renders judgment on an issue related to what your own little criminals do. Are you hard?

If only women's sexual characteristics weren't out front for all to see. Everyone assumes, incorrectly, that her hard nipples herald sexual arousal. But baggy Republican suits conceal a willy hardened by cruelty. After the cameras left and the room emptied, did those guys do that stiff walk Niles Crane does when Daphne's just made a joke about her knickers?

I think we should be told.

23. Things I have lost

A pair of brown suede gloves with Musketeer gauntlets that went up to the elbow, appliquéd with black embroidered curlicues. Suspected site of loss: a gutter beside an outdoor bank machine. S. parks far from the curb to protect his hubcaps, though not the boots of his wife. But it saddens me that I should lose the quality that attracts older men to younger women, the fact that younger women will actually say things like "Oh honey, you park so good." I used to say that to him, and still do, despite the loss of the gloves. Those gloves were a bit over the top anyway.

A huge pair of pearl earrings so heavy that people were always warning me they were about to drop off my lobes. I hurled them at the wall during an argument and discovered what's inside fake pearls, like what's inside golf balls: nothing very interesting or pretty. But at least they were irretrievably shattered. Unlike the gloves, I know that no other woman is wearing them.

I wrote a fan letter to the late brave wonderful Jessica Mitford once, she of *The American Way of Death* and *Hons and Rebels* and that marriage to Winston Churchill's nephew, Esmond Romilly. She sent back the most elegant engraved notecard, the size of a recipe card, on which she thanked me for my kind praise and mentioned that she had just returned from England with the flu, "STAMINA at its lowest." She wrote just as she spoke then, with that upper-class habit of emphasizing words at random. The card went missing ten years ago. I would never have been mad enough to throw it away, except by accident. I am convinced it sits in a file somewhere. I want it, oh I want it. She was a brave, good woman who faced the death of a husband and an eleven-year-old son, persecution by the U.S. government and the Nazi-brand fascism of much of her blood family with immense courage and humour.

I follow the Moscow rule of shopping as laid out by the shopping guide writer Suzy Gershman. If you see it, buy it. Moscow isn't the kind of place where you can comparison shop. How I wish I had bought that triangular black velvet purse attached to the wrist by a velvet band that I saw in a little shop on the rue de Castiglione in Paris. I call this the French rule of shopping. You'll see that beauty only once. The French are implacable. Its loss will haunt you. Mistaken purchases you can toss away. But the things you didn't buy crowd your attic brain. Two years later I go into the store and confess to the owner. Always buy it at the time, she says. I buy a brown velvet shawl trimmed with crumpled satin. Sadly, I only love it 90 percent, not 100 percent like the purse.

My great-aunt Ida had a desk made out of an old-fashioned piano. It had hefty round piano legs and stubby proportions that I've never seen since, a perfect balance of fat kid legs and luscious battered dark wood. It belonged to my grandfather, perhaps, or some other branch of the family. Even as a child, I yearned for that desk. After my great-aunt died, my mother did an unusually thoughtful thing, given what a ratlike teenager I was at the time: she offered to buy it from the relative who had it willed to him. He said no. I feel this book would have been better written on that desk.

I sit on my deck looking at the huge oaks that fill the gardens and a small park behind the house. I look at the highest leaf on the tallest oak. I know I will never touch that leaf, no matter how long I live or what efforts I make with Hydro trucks and buckets. I like looking at it, knowing the matter is out of my hands. I didn't lose the leaf. It is beyond me and that's that and I don't care, but whether I care or not, it's still not to be. That this is true of a million other objects doesn't even register.

I have never lost a woman friend. When it became necessary, I always dropped them, cut them off and never missed them. Is this a precautionary weakness in me or simple common sense? I have enough trouble with female enemies; I will not be treated badly by a female friend. It's a rule.

24. A thing I won't lose

My body has a boundary. Never be vaccinated at the office. The employer, no matter how he plays with your brain, listens in on your phone calls and reads your emails, must never be allowed inside your physical body. A simple rule but a good one.

25. Fragrances

The united non-smell of every single thing when you have a cold, which kills the taste buds and takes away 40 percent of enjoyment.

Fragrances, once allowed to flavour commercial products, are never the same. Lemon now puts me in mind of cleaning products, pine of unventilated rooms. Manufacturers are trying to steal vanilla from me, but I shan't let them.

A beautiful French diplomat, exquisitely dressed, holds court in a room whose walls are lined with buttercup-coloured silk. As we speak animatedly on the unemployment chaos that will result if too many Eastern European countries enter the EU—we both regretfully deplore the eventual admittance of Albania and its cousins—I can smell his sharp armpit odour which unquestionably has been allowed to build for several days. Good for him. This is the true sensual France. I feel like Tolstoy, obsessed as always, rejoicing at finding a hint of Russian peasant in a Frenchified St. Petersburg drawing room. This is the real thing, he'd say.

Getting off a plane at the southern edge of Canada's north and smelling the combined force of millions of acres of forest coming at me like Dunsinane Wood. But it is not conifers, precisely, or even wood. It is sawn wood from the local mill.

The odour of jet fuel upon takeoff. It still excites me after all these years, even on brief flights to mundane places that one makes out of sheer duty.

Red Door, by Elizabeth Arden, which I have worn for years, even before it was discovered to be the perfume worn by the prostitute giving Hugh Grant fellatio as he was arrested in his car in Los Angeles.

So Pretty, by Cartier, which I enjoy even as I marvel at the childishness of the obvious joke. Question: What's the perfume you're wearing? Answer: It's So Pretty. Question: Yeah, but what is it? You'd expect something more sophisticated from Cartier, but there you are.

Jo Malone sells a body lotion that smells so strongly of grapefruit that it defies logic. There is no circumstance that would have me rolling in sliced grapefruits, no way for this perfume to be plausible. Women shouldn't pay to smell of food.

The violent and stupid Otto in *A Fish Called Wanda,* snorting at his armpit for moral support as he goes off to beat someone senseless.

Choking clouds of hairspray drift from salons as you walk by the doorway, the smell of industrial beauty.

All high schools smell alike. It comes from the miles of lockers. Am I insane or is this erotic?

26. Personal rites of passage

We all define wealth differently. After being raised on a postwar diet that always sounds to me like four people at dinner fighting over one boiled egg, S. recalls his badge of triumph on the road to a moneyed future: ordering the mixed grill at the New Inn in Fremington, North Devon.

After the student poverty years of agonizing over whether I could afford a Virago paperback (I particularly remember Antonia White's *Beyond the Glass,* which was all of $7.95 and had on its cover a stunning Clausen painting of a young girl in a state of anxiety. I decided against it), I now buy books wildly, thoughtlessly and never count the cost. As Woolf said, "Spend freely and trust in your capacity to earn more." I buy books the way the great American humorist Jean Kerr said she bought underpants: the way other people buy gin. (She had six children.) My home is insulated with double layers of books that coat the walls and reach the ceiling in every room. Money is good.

27. Objects that speak

When I travel, I always photograph my hotel room, particularly the bed. It's a form of diary, although not as bleak as Douglas Coupland's photographs of empty modernist airports. But it's not the bed that I'm celebrating, it's everything around and outside the bed that isn't in the photograph because it's too extensive to even try. The Bed and All That Implies, Hotel Ukraina, Moscow, 1976.

The International Language of the Illiterate directs us to a men's toilet and a women's toilet, the only difference in the sign being the triangle around the woman's lower half that signifies a skirt. But women have lost the habit of skirts. Sometimes I have to say it out loud—Skirt = Woman—to avoid entering the wrong room.

There are many fine writers, although not of fiction. But there are not many fine modern photographers; otherwise I would not be able to name so many: Sebastiao Salgado, Don McCullin, Jane Bown, Nan Goldin, Richard Avedon, Rineke Dijkstra. Roland Barthes said there was a "punctum," the unintentionally remarkable part of a photo or movie still that "rises from the scene, shoots out of it like an arrow, and pierces me." It's a trigger. It gives him a shock. I know exactly what he means. What mystifies me is how rarely this happens, how the world of photography has such a tiny pool of genuine talent that photos rarely hit you the way a spear gun hits a shark. Unlike acting, where the talent pool is so huge that the untalented can rise and the brilliant can waitress for decades and no court will redress the wrong.

House burning down? The one object I would carry out without doubt would be a Mother's Day card from my little stepdaughter, back when she hardly knew me. It reads: "Vilets are peurpel. Rosese are reb. Hope yo have a nice moser's day." And then because of joint custody and her not knowing if she'll see me on the actual day, she reassures me. "I comme [she attends a French school] to give this givet to you." I have never been able to get over the sociability and kindness of this little girl because at this point, I wasn't even her actual step-moser, just some bint her father had brought home.

28. Things that are crap

Dishes made out of food. A doughnut shop sells a hearty soup in a bread bowl, literally a hollowed-out bun with a stupid little cap sliced off the top. Are they trying to save on china? Did someone dream of a sandwich with a filling that oozed out, and a light bulb went on over their head? I cannot nail down the precise reason, but there is something disgusting about it, like reusable medical equipment. Also, what if you eat the bowl first?

Begging letters from a hospital where a friend died. You donated once. And then you are deluged, but in a 1950s wifey style: the honorific is never Ms. but Mrs. And they assume you've taken your husband's entire name. Princess Andrew or Mrs. Bob Builder, they write in their stopped-time Catholic way. No such person exists, and why should they assume that my dear friend had restricted his friendships to good Catholic types?

29. Things that should be crap but are brilliant

I love the British left-wing politician Tony Benn. He started out life as Anthony Wedgwood Benn, was involuntarily turned into

Viscount Stansgate when his father died, and then rejected the title and turned himself into Tony Benn, which, as he points out in *Free at Last!,* the most recent volume of his political diaries, won't help his stuck-with-the-title grandson much. The poor child is one day old, and if something unfortunate happens to Tony or Tony's son on the way home, someone's going to have to diaper someone called Viscount Stansgate. Without laughing.

No, that's not the brilliant bit. Benn has a CD out, *Tony Benn's Greatest Hits,* in which his best speeches are made alongside a wonderful soundtrack by Charles Bailey, who has dreadlocks. No, it's not rap or funk, it's just, well, frankly, the kind of low-key, beautiful hypnotic music that I could have sex to. (I often play porn in hotel rooms just for the soothing sax music.) And it makes the speeches listenable. It's not that I'm not interested in Benn protesting that male vicars in the Church of England should not be paid compensation for the vile experience of being forced to work with female vicars (astonishingly, this is true), but wouldn't anyone prefer to listen to PJ Harvey rather than political speeches on a wet Sunday afternoon? Still, Benn's *Greatest Hits* is my favourite CD right now. Also, he talks like Churchill and he's handsome, the elderly George Clooney of the British Labour Party.

Nothing makes my heart sink more than letters from readers correcting my grammar. My grammar is pretty much perfect. I only mess things up deliberately, to put in a line from an obscure country song that I know some good, hurtin' reader will pick up instantly or to make up a whole new word that the English language suddenly requires. But yes, grammar matters. Lynne Truss, a fine writer who managed to get a funny novel out of life at a gardening magazine, has written a book on grammar called *Eats, Shoots and Leaves: The Zero Tolerance Approach to Punctuation.*

The title is explained thus: A panda goes into a bar, orders a sandwich, eats it and fires a gun into the air. The bartender asks him what he's doing and he shoves a book on the bar and says, "This is a badly punctuated wildlife manual. Look me up." The bartender does so and finds, under Panda: Large, black-and-white, bear-like mammal native to China. Eats, shoots and leaves. Of course, the whole idea is stolen from an old Aussie joke: Why is your boyfriend like a wombat? Answer: Because he eats, roots and leaves.

Thanks, Lynne. But I'm very attached to dashes. If you prefer ellipses, we may come to blows. (If I may make the most obscure remark ever, Jacqueline Kennedy Onassis was dash-happy. The woman was mad for them. I gaze in awe as her letters are quoted in her many biographies. They are practically one horizontal line.)

30. First days at work

First days at work are always horrid. Where are the toilets? Where is the photocopier? My desk has no phone. But this one set a record.

I arrive at the front desk and find that my name is not on a list of staffers to be allowed in the building. They call upstairs and my kind supervisor comes downstairs and takes me to the security office. A real bastard of a private agency cop tells me he has no record of me and demands to see my letter of employment. I'm about to hand it over when I realize it includes my salary. I'm not going to tell you my salary, I say (I don't doubt it would mean the entire building would know instantly). I know I am about to cry, as this is a job I never wanted anyway, and my supervisor drags me into a nearby washroom where I do cry, quite lavishly. I'll deal with him, she says fiercely, and when I go back to his office, he silently takes my picture and gives me my pass which I am to hang around my neck. Yep, it is a picture of me holding back tears, not very well.

Finally, I'm in my cubicle, shaking, and notice a man sitting opposite, very casually with his legs up on the desk in the cubicle. A photographer is standing on the desk snapping away.

Yes, it is Scott Adams, the man who created Dilbert, the comic strip that painted office life as it really was: a scorched cubicle hell, a factory farm of misery. The man is a genius, but he is also a millionaire who no longer works in a cubicle.

His publicist introduces him to me, as I have just written a column about his new book on corporate weasels. I look at him silently. I have backed myself into the corner of my cubicle. My face crumples. "This is my first day," I tell him. "The security guard made me cry and then he took a picture of me. It's laminated now."

Adams looks at my pass and winces. He talks to me quietly and gently. He gives me a copy of his weasel book and signs it. "It's Heather, isn't it?" He remembers my name because who forgets a frightened face with its eyes all buried and tragic? He is terribly kind.

Later in the day, I ask where the washroom is. Only one cubicle (cubicle!) is free, and I flush the toilet before I use it because it has paper floating in it. It explodes, pouring water and shreds of excrement all over the floor and vacating the other stalls. What are the odds, eh?

In the end, I quit the job.

Bill Bryson describes hiking the Appalachian Trail this way: "No engagements, commitments, obligations or duties; no special ambitions and only the smallest, least complicated of wants; you exist in a tranquil tedium serenely beyond the reach of exasperation." That summed up all that the job required of me, "the willingness to trudge." But I couldn't even do that.

31. Times when one should be on one's guard

When people who want to hire you tell you a private anecdote; some moment of humiliation, say, to show they are on your level. Which in itself is insulting. When you say yes to the job, they slowly turn off any connection with you as if they were nurses and you were hooked up to an oxygen tank.

32. Things that bedevil one

The office sends me an email warning me that I use the new computer system at my peril, it being much more "mouse-dependent" than whatever preceded it. I have no idea what they are talking about. After much investigation, it appears that my co-workers are going to be doing more one-handed work, mouse-clicking rather than typing (but why?), and the company will have to pay stroppy employees large sums of money if they injure their primary wrist.

1) The solution to this is, one supposes, to announce that masturbation is banned and anyone who develops carpal tunnel syndrome will be known by their hairy palms. 2) No one I know there does enough work to injure anything except their hindquarters. 3) Whoever messes with the English language to the extent of inventing "mouse-dependent" should be shot. My niece is deeply in love with her gerbil named Nutmeg. Is she now gerbil-dependent? Must she get counselling when Nutmeg loses her tail as gerbils tend to do, leading to a disgusting discovery in a dusty corner months down the road?

Having just read Paul Burrell's *A Royal Duty,* it appears that there is not a single decent person in the British royal family nor among anyone they consort with nor in the vile and viperous Spencer family. Diana was the only nice one and she's dead. They're both huge families. Is it coincidence? Is it heredity? Money? Drunkenness?

We read of Burrell asking Prince Charles if he truly expected him to lie on his behalf, and Charles, puce, throwing a book at Burrell's head and saying, "Yes, I am! I am the Prince of Wales, and I will be the king!! So yes. YES!" Serpents all.

And another troubling thing: the latest royal scandal that dare not speak its name. I think it's that Mrs. Parker Bowles, partner of Il Tampolino, is a man. S. thinks the Duke of Edinburgh has been sleeping with this same Parker Bowles. Someone else says they have a love child, now grown up. Or then again, if anyone's secretly a man, it's Princess Anne. But then I see a picture of the wife of the huge piece of rough trade that is "Princess" Charles's former valet Marc Bolland, the man who held HRH's hospital specimen bottle as he peed, and I do hope not the organ itself. I understand completely. For she is the butchest woman I've ever seen.

The answer to a mystery is always the simplest: Is the scandal that Charles is, in fact, a woman?

33. Things that would be pleasing in a sick way

Sexual intercourse with the men who pop up for fifteen minutes in the course of world events. I would be unable to concentrate. Even as the hawklike countenance of French Foreign Minister Dominique de Villepin was poised over one's face, I'd be wondering if he's a "corkscrew" man. (Young women are said to leave the office of Jacques Chirac having re-clothed themselves so hastily that their stockings corkscrew along their legs.) And Donald Rumsfeld's Vitalis-streaked hair and narrowed eyes: Would he wear those half-glasses for the really close work? And at a crucial moment, would one look down at his head and think of the tortured at Guantánamo and remember the one-eyed countenance of General Paul Aussaresses, eighty-four, the French general who remembers his tortures and executions of young Algerian men in the 1960s as necessary and, one suspects, pleasurable? (He was fined seventy-five hundred euros.)

The trick is to close the mind, with wine or drugs or stupidity, chop the endless links to what these men do for a living. I mean, they're only one-night stands, if that. But I have never been able to shut the damn thing off, not even during sex.

34. The worst people in the world

The worst people in the world are the Literals. I once wrote a column purporting to sympathize with a bloated bombastic American radio show blowhard who was addicted to the constipating painkiller OxyContin. If you hadn't been to the bathroom since 1999, you'd be cranky too, I said. A reader then sent me a detailed letter explaining that it would be medically impossible for this man not to void his bowels for years at a time. Ruth Rendell has built a career writing about grubby demented little freaks like this. I wonder if my reader is a murderer.

35. Reasons not to marry creative types

(with thanks to Phil Baker, brilliant author of *The Book of Absinthe*)

Verlaine's parents loved him. His mother had had a series of miscarriages before giving birth. The problem was that she kept the fetuses pickled, in jars, around the house. The modern stance advocates giving people "time to grieve" but there are limits surely. I'm not saying this is the source of Verlaine's problems, but can you imagine the domestic scene, especially as the absinthe kicked in? Harsh accusations are made. "You'd like to see me in formaldehyde, too!" "Pas vrai, Paul, I love you best. But ever since you started lounging with that nogoodnik Arthur Rimbaud, you've been impossible." And what do you get a sibling jar for Christmas? In the end, he smashed them all in a fit of temper.

Oscar Wilde, exiled in Paris, wrote "The Morgue yawns for me. I go and look at my zinc bed there." And yes he did. We all know the hell Wilde went through. The half hour he spent at the train station in Clapham Junction, where he was jeered at and spat on by a gathering crowd, would have done me in. But would I visit my slab-to-be, even in extremis? Oh, perhaps.

I think of the poet Ernest Dowson as a glamorous figure. After all, he was only faithful to Cynara in his fashion but his fashion was pretty glammed up and I like that. But eating, bathing, wearing clean clothes, not spewing on people—eventually it was all beyond his abilities after he got hooked on the absinthe.

Not that you would have married Salvador Dali anyway (think of all the places a woman doesn't want crusts of moustache wax), but he tried to enhance his charms by shaving his armpits to make them bleed and coating his body with boiled fish glue and goat manure. Perhaps this attracted female Surrealists. Who can say?

Or Arthur, Paul's friend, who not only had head lice but kept them so that he could fling them at passing priests. Sonia Orwell used to spit at nuns when she saw them in the street. I understand this perfectly and like both of these brave and splendid people. But thank heavens one of Rimbaud's friends, Antoine Cros, came back to the bar that time and noticed his drink was bubbling. That can't be good, he thought. Rimbaud had put sulphuric acid in it.

36. Why I'm glad Cros didn't drink it

This same Cros wrote a children's poem called "The Salt Herring," which Baker describes as follows: "A rhyme about nothing, it is the story of a blank white wall against which a man leans a ladder and bangs in a nail, tying a string to the nail and then tying a dried herring to the string, which continued to twist in the wind ever after." I know what you're thinking—perhaps he did have that drink and wrote the poem straight after. But "The Salt Herring" strikes me as a metaphor for a lot of things: Jeffrey Archer, almost every job I have ever had, Romania under Ceausescu, the previously mentioned Hoon. Dried salt herrings slapping against a wall. It's a phrase that you know will come in handy.

37. The effort it takes to avoid advertising

The effort it takes to avoid advertising has become so immense that perhaps it is counterproductive. I click on Comedy Central's online clips from *The Daily Show with Jon Stewart* and turn my head away and shut down the speakers while an ad runs before the clip. I don't read buses. I tear out huge advertising sections of *The New Yorker* and discover to my fury that I have destroyed the last page of the only thing worth reading, a David Sedaris story or something by Seymour M. Hersh. I avoid billboards, subway signs and elevator screens, I mute TV ads, don't watch movies in theatres, send all email directly to the junk bin and sift for real stuff, use folded Kleenex rather than bookstore bookmarks, deal briskly with telemarketers and dispose of anything that looks like junk mail which was why I accidentally failed to pay my gas bill for three months. "This isn't like me," I told the man when I called him about his polite letter.

The odd thing is that I shop like mad, so much so that I am actually paid by a publication to write brief essays about stuff I've purchased. But there is an inverse relationship between a product that advertises and how likely I am to buy it. I like to find things on my own.

As for the horror of living in a part of the planet so prosperous that I am close to being overrun with stuff, too much stuff, useless stuff—look, how many sets of sheets should I have? I have ten. It's a lot for one bed. Inevitably, I favour two sets and the other eight sit patiently in the linen closet.

I have a special large cabinet for my underwear. It has twenty-four separate drawers. I use four.

38. Hunting the detail

Right after the 2003 blackout in parts of Canada and the U.S. Eastern Seaboard, I read on the wire about a Texas doctor who was getting on an elevator in the hospital where he worked when the doors closed on him, crushing his shoulders. The elevator took off. He was decapitated. There was a woman in the elevator at the time, and she was being treated for shock.

Three things struck me: a) In the list of possible awful deaths, this man had truly lucked out, b) That was one person who could have used the electrical blackout we were having but was unfortunate enough to live in Texas, independent of the main American electrical grid, and c) The woman in the elevator was left with something: Was it the head or the body? After days of searching, I was able to discover the answer to this last question about which the world was curious but which no reporter was willing to supply. The elevator went up, and his body fell into the empty shaft. So she got the head, at least the bit from the jaw up. I never understand the chastity of reporting. Why do I have to do the investigative work?

The inquest revealed that the doctor was dead drunk. It was 9:30 in the morning. And he was on duty. Later, they figured out that the elevator wiring had one small—but crucial—flaw.

Apparently, Germans were gripped by a murder trial where a man advertised on the internet for a victim he could kill and eat. And yes, there was a Mr. Right. First, he allowed the killer to cut his willy off and they sat and ate the cooked dis-member. Then the murder took place, but I don't care. I only want to know one thing. How did he cook it? Boiled or steamed? Served in a bun with ketchup? As usual, most newspapers are too polite to tell me. After much searching, I find out he flambéed it. So it was served *bleu* then, was it?

I cannot forget the rosy red rings that Jackie recalled seeing on the inside of JFK's skull as it flew into the air. Sometimes I wonder if the increasing coarseness of popular culture dates back to the Zapruder film and the number of times U.S. citizens were made to watch casually as a man's head exploded.

A doctor tells me that the cervix feels like the end of one's nose. How many other parts of the body can be twinned in this way?

39. I have fond memories

I have fond memories of the rundown polytech where my husband and I first met when he was teaching and I was studying journalism as a frantic means of finding a use for an M.A. in English. At the time, there wasn't anything about Virginia Woolf I didn't know, and there wasn't anything in newspapers he hadn't done on three continents, but we were both at loose ends.

Polytechs remind me of the University of North-Eastern England (motto: We Take Anyone) in one of the funniest novels ever written, Mil Millington's *Things My Girlfriend and I Have Argued About,* and David Lodge's classic fictional redbrick university Rummidge. I make no connections here, but Millington works at the University of Wolverhampton, Lodge teaches at the University of Birmingham, and my little polytech and its fellows are now universities, or are linked with universities, where I suspect I cannot teach without a Ph.D. that qualifies me to do or supervise academic research.

Of what does this consist in journalism? Reading old newspapers? I feel sad for a place that was once proud to claim that it had links with the industry that found students paying jobs across the country. Are we going to have students going all Bridesheady and keeping teddy bears in the high school lockers that line the corridors of former polytechnical institutes? Mutton dressed as lamb, a raddled old prostitute who keeps her lamps very dim indeed. It was one way for the government to claim more students were being university educated: turn anything into a university including the subway station and the local Payless ShoeSource.

Journalism isn't a profession. It's a craft. You do it fast and well, like plumbing. Some do it fast and brilliantly. Then it's called brilliant plumbing.

40. McDonald's' cheap plastic job lot

McDonald's' cheap plastic job lot of crap toylets they served with their Happy Meals lured my nieces into a trailer park world from which they will be extracted only with great difficulty. For instance, I call my niece and ask her what she'd like me to buy her in Paris. Perhaps a lovely gown from Repetto, the store for ballerinas? A Babar extravaganza? "Nintendo," she says. I lie, and say French Nintendo wouldn't plug in here.

I tried to lure her into a distant love of Paris with the Madeline books. Unfortunately, I made the mistake of coming back crowing that Parisian schoolchildren do indeed march in two straight lines.

It's not much different from the classic children's Buddy System, but they were wearing uniforms. She was horrified. A regulated universe. It's bad enough sitting in a classroom in desks that line up.

Then I mailed her a card from Paris, some Morisot painting perhaps of schoolgirls skipping alone. "That's not a straight line,' my little niece sneered. Smirk. Snicker. "It's straight in a conceptual sense," I said feebly. "It's not straight," she said flatly. Paris held no fears for her after that. No interest either, now that she knew its alleged orderly tortures of children were mere inventions.

41. I visit my girlfriend

I visit my girlfriend at her weekend home in the country, feeling very much like the city mouse. They own a farm with barns and guest houses, miniature horses, cornfields, kingfishers, a "pond" (Jennifer, where I come from, that's called a lake), herons, sturdy nature-made walking sticks strewn about the woodland paths and water pumped from a well. Weirdly, they have a glamorous (negative-edge, as it's known in the business) pool which creates the impression with its glass wall that the water is flowing into a vast cornfield with Biblical abundance. I first encountered this now fairly common style of pool at the Regent (now InterContinental) Hotel, and kept having flashbacks that we were filling up Hong Kong Harbour whenever we splashed. City mouse.

Her children are James, three, Buzz, five, and Nicola, nine. Like their parents, they are good-looking, especially Nicky with her chimney sweep eyelashes, and the psychological sexual force exerted within the house by so many winsome people is unusual. I have never lived in a beauty magnet city like Los Angeles and feel vaguely drugged, pumped up by an invisible power.

I adore other people's children but know nothing of boys, nothing. As it turns out, the only difference is that boys are turbines of mischief and their hugs are more emphatic than those of girls. Otherwise, it's the same. Both sexes cry when they step on a tiny plastic helicopter buried in the carpet. I work hard at concealing my complete approval of everything these children do, as it can't be good for them, but secretly I convince Buzz that I am one of his aunts.

At one point I see Jennifer in the pool embracing black-haired Buzz in the curve of one arm while her other arm holds his legs. She spins, whirling him like a windmill. She has this extraordinary smile of love and complete encircling fondness as she looks down at him. I don't think I have seen this expression on a human face before. She is the Pietà with the significant difference that Jesus has been replaced by Buzz. I knew Jennifer in her twenties. I never thought I would see her beatified so young.

They are, I suspect, rich. Steve is a financier and I feel slightly uncomfortable in his presence, feeling he is tolerating me and my socialist views for his wife's sake. There, I've said it, I who was raised never to discuss money. Wealth gives them an ease, as extreme wealth would not.

I know openly rich people who radiate dissatisfaction and hostility. There is always someone with more money and this eats at them. So, no, the magic ingredient isn't money. Jennifer reminds me of Rosamond Lehmann and the idyllic childhood described in her novel *Dusty Answer*. She has a good mind, is relentlessly clever, has a powerful sexuality and enjoys creating an amplitude around her, as I do. The sangria flows, the books are plentiful and scattered, the beds are soft.

She is a marathon runner. That's it. I shall jog my way into superior womanhood.

42. Things that explain a lot

The British politician Tony Benn, who has weathered the scorn of the right wing, decades in British Parliament, severe illness and the death of his wife without ever wavering in his beliefs and courage, says that when he was a little boy, his mother would put him to bed every night saying "And tomorrow will be a wonderful day." She thus erased that day's woes and wiped the slate clean for the next day's happiness. Cannot imagine this happening to me as a child. Well, if today was dreadful, tomorrow will be absolute shite would be the Scottish way of preparing a child for the morrow. This doesn't have to be said; it hangs unspoken in the air.

43. In the belly of the office

Complaints of a co-worker

Corns, sinuses, spine, rashes (entire body), mouth, teeth, skin, public transit, poverty, women who complain about sexual harassment, non-whites. Spends her days filled with rage. Hasn't had sex for eight years, she says. Divorced. Desperate.

Likes of a co-worker

Guns, codeine, stun guns, smuggled cigarettes, no-name booze, Buffalo, whatever's on special in the cafeteria today. Biggest concern in life: parking.

Drinking heavily. Suddenly he turns savage at a staff dinner. He goes to the washroom. Time passes. Someone goes to check but he isn't there. All that is left is a torn-off wing mirror in the parking lot. The crash, the arrest, the bail, all that comes later.

Dislikes of a co-worker

Women, non-whites, homosexuals, liberals, neighbours, people who are successful, people who work at his place of work, people who work at other places of work, his wife, his little boy on Ritalin, his other little boy who has pulled all his own hair out, house, car, town where he lived, Jews, city where he lives, mother, horse he owned that went bald. Likes: big band music, Jack Russell terriers, cleaning ears with finger, cleaning fingernails with scissors and letter openers.

Heartfelt declarations of a worker

Jonathan Franzen says, "In twenty-five years, I have yet to find a work situation that isn't somehow about family, or loyalty, or sex, or guilt, or all four. I'm beginning to think I never will." Sound familiar?

A man who worked at the Westray Mine in Nova Scotia where twenty-six workers died in a terrible accident in 1992 used to shift his rearview mirror as he drove away from the place. It was such an awful place to work that the sight of it looking at him as he drove away was unbearable.

In *Refusal Shoes,* Tony Saint's 2003 novel about working as an Immigration Officer at Heathrow, "the first buffet of Terminal C depression slams into him. It is a unique sensation, like being cored."

The best thing I have ever seen in a workplace was a computer monitor bursting into flames. It then burned away quietly to itself, the orange flames licking at the beige plastic while an odd-smelling smoke filled the room. We sat hopefully, waiting for the fire to move from computer to computer via an endless tangle of wire. Perhaps we would be required to set our own computers on fire to create a barrier the flames couldn't leap, as they do in Australian bush fires, but to our sorrow, this request was not made. The whole thing was strangely restful and made us happy.

The jobs I've held down always make me think of John Cleese's line in the movie *Clockwise* as he sits by the side of the road, physically incapacitated and mentally destroyed by his effort to get somewhere intact and on time. Something like, "I don't mind the despair, it's the hope I can't stand."

44. Things you simply cannot stick

The French show their contempt for artists I worship and they dismiss. Raoul Dufy's magnificent *La Fée Electricité,* completed in 1937, and works from other artists of his era cannot be seen by the public at the Musée d'Art Moderne de la Ville de Paris. It is not open to visitors as an exhibition of Scandinavian art is being set up. It will take a week to do this. One young woman, gasping that she came to Paris just to see those paintings, collapses on the front steps in shock and frustration.

On your next visit to the city, you are reluctantly permitted to see Dufy's work. First you must travel past a work of art, a water exhibit that is a tower of glass shelves displaying bottled water from around the world. Yes, that's a nice-looking Ty Nant all right. Are they mad? When you reach the oval gallery, you are prevented from getting closer to Dufy's enormous detailed watercolours by a pile of old knitting on the floor. There are skeins of pastel nylon wool and knitted things that look like ratty legwarmers. I express my feelings when I leave by giving the thing a good kick and a mix with both feet. I do hope this destroys the integrity of the piece but I'd be surprised if it were apparent even to the artist. We complain about French rudeness, but they have the same attitude to their compatriots as they do to visitors. Only now are they revising the official attitude to Claude Monet.

45. In the hotel elevator

In the hotel elevator in Paris, I embrace S., not for any particular reason and not sexually, more of a hug. Next to us, the middle-aged Frenchman in the mirrored elevator laughs drunkenly and says to me, *"Tu es pressé?"* meaning "You can't wait to have sex?" He grasps my hand, behind S.'s back, so that S. cannot see him do it.

Despite the sterling French record on this sort of thing, a landmark has been reached. I was in my husband's arms! We discuss this later with some awe, mixed with disgust.

A man at work once said to me of another reporter, "You really want to fuck him. Admit it." I was so angry I did that rigid thing where rage makes even my bendy veins stand up straight. I never spoke to him again and once when he put his hand on my shoulder I actually shuddered as though he were viral.

For here's the odd thing: I love S. I love him more with each year that passes. But this isn't the accepted spin on marriage. People can't understand that I will not allow them to insult S. He is mine.

Public loyalty to a spouse is no longer fashionable. I meet women who casually go to strip clubs to pick out a male stripper for their girlfriend's "stag," a man who'll end the evening stirring their drinks with his willy, and all I can think of is that if I hired a male stripper, S. would have me disinfected and then find me a rooming house in which to end my days. I would have done the same to him. Aw. Okay, I would let him live in the basement.

46. Things that just might not be worth the effort

Christmas. Baking, decorating, log stacking, testing outdoor lights, buying new ones, destroying shrubs with new outdoor lights, house cleaning, sending cards to people of whom only five will truly be touched, menu planning, list making, choking the fridge with food, shopping, wrapping, hiding things, tree choosing/dragging/decorating, filling stockings, faking delight, concealing fury when it's clear the gift will be exchanged, taking photos, setting the table, being disappointed by hugely expensive crackers that don't bang. S. cooks the meal beautifully although he no longer carves the goose at the table after one Christmas when he found himself cradling the big greasy thing with his fingers up its fundament.

All this is done to give the children a feeling of amplitude I didn't have at Christmas because it wasn't expected by my parents' generation or, to be honest, my own. Is it worth it? I won't know till they're fifty. And I'll be dead then surely.

47. The same holiday seen through happier eyes, in my diary

Pleasures of Christmas

1. Smell of cinnamon and cranberry potpourri, lotions, soaps, bath beads, Jil Sander No. 4, pine tree
2. The look of happiness on my darling's face
3. Food: roast goose, sherbet, chocolate, truffles, Georges DuBoeuf white wine, sake
4. Fires breaking up wood
5. Flannel sheets and nightgowns
6. Gleam of lights, wrapping paper, camera flashes
7. Music: Van Morrison's blues, Bob Marley, The Barra MacNeils
8. Purple satin slips, white lace body suits

9. Colours: red, green, gilt, silver
10. Nancy Mitford's letters
11. The warmth and love of my well-clad stepchildren

What a feeble list. It reads like an ad. Was I wibbly with mulled wine when I wrote it? Even Julie Andrews had better favourite things in *The Sound of Music*. Booze makes you gloss over mundanity. Imagine listing red and green as a pleasure. Even if I liked those colours, my sober self would dress them up a little to convince myself that they are truly fine. Scarlet and fragrant green, I'd say. Sober, reading myself blitzed, I regard my former self the way I would a dim but good-natured cousin I see once every few years just to be nice.

48. Things about cleaning

There's elegant cleaning, which means putting lavender water in your iron or the washing machine, that marvellous front-loading energy-saving thing so huge that it could wash your lawn so that you could unfold it, damply and nicely, in the front garden of a morning.

And then there's the hard graft of cleaning up after a teenager and her admittedly filthy roommates. Are you sure you want to do this, they say. There's bugs in the kitchen. Oh, a few flies, you think. We'll soon fix that.

And then you see the place. The giant metal garbage can hasn't been emptied in months and its bag long ago gave way to leave a lining of milky coffee, bits of cat food, hair, mould and black things on the newspaper that was once placed hopefully on the bottom of the can. Even when the bag is removed, dripping, into its second bag, and the can is scraped and filled with hot water and bleach, a cloud of small unidentifiable black bugs hovers in the cupboard and indeed the entire kitchen. They are, I think, fruit flies. There are thirty-six plates coated in fuzzy tomato sauce and onions and dozens of beer bottles with cigarette butts floating in their bottom yellow inch, glasses coated with red pockmarks and cat food everywhere. The recycling has been magnificent but for the fact that nothing cardboard or glass was ever taken anywhere, merely stored in cupboards. There is a lot of it. The insects die but not anywhere I can see them, which worries me.

Some kind of mealy material, possibly dead mice, has pushed the oven some distance from the wall and the drawer at the bottom clanks along the floor as it does in all dwellings of this type. No drawer may ever roll on its track in such a place; it's symbolic.

Orange goo coats the walls of the fridge and the freezer. What leaks in a freezer? A freezer is surely the only place where nothing leaks, as it freezes into place. That's what makes it a freezer. We have a category error here of long duration. And why are there huge chunks of bagged ice but no ice cubes? If I chisel some ice into a glass, am I welcoming tapeworms into my person or was this chunk merely used on the balcony in the winter months for the cats to pee on?

There is a terrible smell upstairs, which I am relieved to discover is only what the cats have expelled, but it has been inside the apartment since it emerged long ago. Yet the harsh lines of dirt are softened somehow. It is cloudy, almost pretty. There is long white cat hair floating through the air, trapped on the lip of each stair covered in a now-brown carpet that has been savaged by teeth and claws. There is enough white hair extant to reconstruct an entire cat should this one meet with misfortune.

Is all this the embodiment of depression or of youth? Or a hostility that expresses itself in a savage passivity even as it slices the noses off teenagers' faces with an impressive finality?

I am cleaning on the hottest day of the year, as a penance for some wrong I committed yet cannot identify. The tragedy, as I leave, is that the apartment is still unspeakable, despite the fact that billions would live in it happily. Dirt doesn't live in the open spaces. It fences itself in. It gets inside things via air currents and crawling legs and hitching rides on animals. Dust combines with cooking to form an all-points glue.

I know now that I could have cleaned those Augean stables. They would have sparkled, albeit just for the next load to come through. This apartment, though—it doesn't gleam, not slightly, not anywhere.

To paraphrase Frost, something there is human that doesn't love dirt. I would eject it from my mechanism but I cannot. I am in shock. I stand under the shower at home, dazed.

49. Things about flowers

After adolescence, gifts of flowers are treasured. They were once beyond the pocketbook, and are beautiful in themselves. Then I read about what we have done in the last twenty years. Flowers are grown in Third World countries where they are doused with artificial fertilizers and pesticides by brown-skinned child labourers whose health matters to no one. They are cut according to the "just in time" manufacturing principle—only as they are ordered by people like me—and flown to North American cities where they command large prices that dwarf the profits of the farmer contracted to grow them. He gets pennies. The flights of these short-lived blossoms turn our city air brown and eat the planet's ozone to a degree that we are only now coming to realize. One looks at one's bundle of roses, freesias and peonies and feels that a serial killer has entered the house. Worse, he was invited and we were thrilled to see him.

S. welcomes me home from a four-day trip with a dozen yellow tulips, my favourite flower. But they flop in their tall vase, curving over in a long arch like a suspension bridge or a dying swan. We look at them. The next day, I cut two inches off their stems and shove them in a taller vase for support. They look like drowning children, heads popping above the water. I cut four inches off them and shove them in a short jug. They still loll about but in an absurd truncated manner. I chuck them out of pity. But we still don't know why they hung their heads and cried in their shirts, sad Lisas.

50. Memories by colour

The pale weak orange of the gum expelled when my friend vomited Fanta in Red Square. We were teenagers on a school trip to Moscow in 1976. Teenagers, like household pets, vomit a lot.

The blue of Princess Diana's bathing suit in the summer of 1997, the year she died, in the Mediterranean. It was the colour of pale turquoise sea, the warmest blue I've ever seen, pure sun on water. It was blue happiness. Clothing of that colour didn't show up on the high street until two or three years later, which revealed the length of the fashion cycle, from top to tail. But emotionally, it felt as though we'd been banned from that colour. Diana wore sea-blue, American prisoners wear orange, and beige, the curse of the modern age, is worn by sofas until it is otherwise decreed.

Penguins used to have strictly orange spines, Viragos had dark leaf green. You'd think they'd have known not to mess around with that.

The heavy crescent-moon shaped navy blue eyeliner on an Intourist guide in Moscow. They were bad-tempered women, shouters all, and I would focus on their eyelids, which never trembled as their lead-lined mouths shouted at me.

My dislike of the colour orange informs my dislike of Halloween. The combination of red and pink in polyester and candy means I'll never appreciate Valentine's Day. The cheap chemical green of St. Patrick's Day screams poverty.

A florist called Black-Eyed Susan's sends me yellow roses and huge blowsy blush-coloured poppies that fade until they are the yellow of the roses. They look like slatterns and I keep them until they rot and slump against each other, living on gin and cigs and shedding sexy pistils.

51. Comforting things

The only thing I truly disliked about being single was being alone while ill. I remember once in university, waking at 5 A.M., shaking and panicky, utterly demoralized. I called my father, who reassured me solely by being my father and a doctor. And then a pop song, "Suddenly" by Olivia Newton-John, came on the radio. Strange how potent cheap music is. The illness faded as I drank water and the memory of the dream vanished. I put on a towelling bathrobe and four blankets with a heating pad. Restored.

Reading an essay by the Japanese novelist Junichiro Tanizaki in which he "follows the brush," writing in a stream of consciousness that seems completely natural. Oil lamps versus electric light, lacquerware, wooden toilet cabinets, soup, Kabuki, Noh, Einstein. Following the brush works. Unlike a *New Yorker* essay where never a tangent is permitted.

52. Things that gain by being painted

Most things. If they were a painting instead of real life, they would look marvellous. A photograph would be even better. You could tear it up.

Fingernails look better painted. Except one recalls the eerie story of JFK Jr.'s wife Carolyn Bessette taking her time over her pedicure, matching the mauve of her nails to the precise shade of her outfit and telling her husband on the phone that his calls were just delaying her even more. Then there were traffic jams. They flew out in their small plane much later than they should have, with little daylight left. And that's what caused the crash into the sea and the subsequent horror of those waterlogged corpses. It's bad enough living through your last moments on earth, even if you aren't aware of the fact. But to spend them in a nail salon where, in retrospect, pale lacquer will be the killing of you ...

53. Things that do not gain by being painted

Invariably the portraits that rich people commission of themselves are insulting to the sitter. The painter had her revenge. Erica Jong poses for a magazine feature in front of her portrait in her overupholstered living room. The portrait looks nothing like her. The flesh is flat and wrinkle-free and her gown floats pointlessly. In real life, she is bug-eyed. There are no Sargents or Tissots around any more to flatter the rich. This is probably the only bug in the wineglass of a rich person in the second millennium.

A woman I rather like, in the sense that she knows what she is after and makes no bones about it, writes a novel in which the main character says she regards her husband as husbands should be regarded. He is a "mighty tree." It was unpleasant enough to contemplate this guy before. Imagine watching that climb into its underpants each morning, I used to think. But now I am visualizing his mighty tree. Is it thick? Or just very long? Is its bark all scrapey and scratchy? The guy seems distinctly unmighty to me, beyond having rich parents. Maybe she just sees him as reliable, a leafy neighbourhood magnet for families bearing picnic baskets. A magnet in a pair of white Y-fronts. Oh lord.

54. Hateful things

Clowns. Absurd garments and a menace concealed behind a coat of white paint and vilely outlined faceholes. Don't let a clown get between you and a door. They all look like John Wayne Gacys to me.

The big dogs owned by foreigners who have bought homes in Venice. It isn't a city for anything big, including dogshit, which is rarely cleaned up and becomes a smeared diminishing landmark for the wandering visitor, as a tree blaze would be in the woods.

The word "cocktail" used to refer to medications.

"Faith-based" to describe Junior Bush's projects that, despite promises, eventually will stop getting money from the government. God will provide.

Trade unions. They keep the oldie mouldies hanging around and block out young people with talent. Inevitably, the work being done goes rotten and the workers with cast-iron job security become indentured servants. Worse, they know it. They despise themselves but can't leave. You can see them sometimes, huddled in corners, smelling stale.

The word "tweak" when used to refer to editing.

55. Splendid things

A heavy Kenneth Jay Lane blue-beaded bracelet in which two lions' heads meet at their orange-tipped noses. The dash of that man!

A golden egg bought at the Victoria & Albert Museum. It sits on my writing desk, implying that I laid it.

A Julia McNeely painting over my bed entitled *Henhouse*. Against a blue background, there are six hens, each in a coop sitting on golden straw, each with a big fat egg so white it has pink tinges. I wasn't thinking food when I hung it there. I was thinking of sexual plenty.

Rose petals scattered in a doorway and out onto a sidewalk in the Marais by a Paris florist wanting to lure customers.

Trade unions. They tell thin-lipped, jargon-loving, pale, cheap-suited management to get stuffed. Sometimes it works. It's a joy to see.

My two-year-old niece lists all those who will go out to dinner with her to celebrate her birthday. "Mummy, Daddy, Grandma, MaMa, Hahoo [me]. All my peoples," she says with great satisfaction.

Suffixes that add mystery and pleasure: Stephen Fry offers his writing for the reader's "perusalment and enjoyage." Similarly, I think of plumbing as flowingness and driety, St. Honoré as a street of exquisite shoppingtons.

56. Fine examples

Simon Schama says the French have a genius for combining nature and human habitation, "landscape and manscape," so that they live in harmony without detracting from each other. He describes the French poetic tradition of "sweet France" where rivers, cultivated fields, orchards, vineyards and woods all co-exist in balance. Villages in the countryside can be heavenly. I'm not sure about this as some of the houses I see in the French countryside are Gallic versions of the jerry-built homes so memorably portrayed in John Boorman's film *Hope and Glory,* about a World War II childhood full of powdered eggs, adult infidelity and an architectural misplacement of windows that calls out for a good bombing. (Yes, I know Betjeman said it first.)

But in the Bois de Boulogne, I take his point. It's full of glades, secret gardens, dells and spinneys, places for picnickers to hide or, famously, for nightcrawlers to have sex. It's unkempt, but cozy enough that it would fit in a children's book. I imagine Kanga and Roo live there. Kew Gardens, the only other park that has ever filled me with joy, is kempt. It's a place of research. Fair enough. But French formality, which has given Paris tiny elaborate knot gardens in courtyards, the Tuileries which is a dressed-up expanse of sand and the Jardins du Luxembourg which is snooty, must bring its citizens pain. In the playground in the Places des Vosges, you can't even walk on the grass! No wonder the well-dressed families with their tablecloths, wicker baskets and exquisite children crowd the Bois. Where else can a Frenchman get grass stains on his Charvet shirt?

57. Things that cannot be compared

My wooden garden shed is a plain old thing. I find some cash in a coat and tart it up, redoing the locks and woodwork and having the thing stained a highly appropriate forest green. The black compressed acrylic tar roof tiles are ripped off and replaced with cedar shingles which I stain, standing on top of the shed, with what I come to realize is not the blue-green last spotted in the ruffled ocean in Monet's brisk afternoon-at-the-seaside painting, *Terrace at Sainte-Adresse,* but a bright blue. Or as a neighbour, who paints everything brownish, put it, "Oh."

Anyway, six months later, I'm in Hervé Chapelier in Paris amid a vast collection of nylon purses in various sizes and styles but most importantly in a range of colours that would make Para Paints or Benjamin Moore Paints feel inadequate. After much fretting, I choose a green bag with a striking base and top trim of exquisite turquoise. Only later do I realize I have spent a large sum of money on a purse that is an exact match for my garden shed.

Worse, it occurs to me that the key accessory is not the purse, but the shed. And you can't take a shed anywhere.

What unconscious forces were at work? In Egypt, Princess Diana dressed to match the camel behind her (my marriage is beige!). John Major dressed to match 10 Downing Street. But what occasion could call out for me matching the place where I store my mulch, garbage and collection of hoes? A wedding in the back garden? The shed would hardly be involved. When will I ever need to casually stand beside my garden shed, carelessly swinging the bag that is its natural neighbour? Should I introduce them? You two have a lot in common, I could say.

Furthermore, the purse is fairly useless but the shed is practicality personified. I know I'd prefer to rescue the shed from a burning building. Could the bag be a stand-in?

Heather, these events must cease.

58. A smell of petroleum prevails throughout

(This is what Bertrand Russell said was the secret of the universe as perceived by a man on laughing gas who could never remember the damn secret once the gas had worn off. Then one day, he just managed to scribble it down. But you knew that.)

In Paris, a smell of dog leavings prevails, in tiny quantities but everywhere, along with little piddles from ridiculously small dogs.

How I long to sniff once more the purple ink used in grade school mimeograph machines in the 1960s.

The smell of a freshly washed baby. Can anything be more vile than manufactured perfume for babies? When our civilization expires, they'll say "This is what did them in. They couldn't stop at perfection."

Things that shouldn't smell but do: Metal. Pharmaceuticals. Stereo speakers. Maps. Water.

59. Harbingers

My neighbour stands on his deck every morning and coughs long and loud. He coughs as though his life depended on it. He has smoked since adolescence and he's almost sixty. He later dies of cancer. The strange thing is, I liked him very much and miss hearing his cough, even though it must have been signalling his death, even to him.

A woman I knew many years ago and now avoid has a reputation for cruelty. She does appalling things to the people who work for her, her decisions are based on whim and she strikes people as "off" somehow. Sometimes she talks nonstop, smokes heavily, makes no sense. Later I hear that she has been diagnosed as manic-depressive and heavy doses of lithium have made her fat. She cannot find a job.

I remember a decades-old conversation with her on a certain subject. It was never repeated. She told me she had an aunt—it was someone connected by blood—who was amazingly energetic. She'd do things fast, cover everything, make decisions, get things done. Then she'd collapse. At the moment she was hospitalized, was mentally ill. I remember my friend's frown as she told me this, but no, I didn't hear a distant bell toll. She must have seen it in herself. I must have seen it too, but it didn't register. Things like bipolar disorder, autism, clinical depression, attention deficit disorder didn't exist until perhaps ten years ago. It wasn't that they weren't discussed. No one had even heard of them.

When I was in high school in the 1970s, I was a Queen Victoria. I had never heard of lesbians. Hadn't heard of gay men either. When a middle-aged woman repeatedly touched my breast "accidentally," when I was sixteen, I just figured she was a little clumsy.

I knew when I saw the big oblong box being slid into the train's luggage compartment that I was in for trouble. HUMAN REMAINS was the label on the outside. It was a bad omen. The cab taking me home from the train station broke down. I wasn't happy but I should have welcomed the delay. My father-in-law was dying, had we but known it. Soon after, S.'s mother died, as did my father. Everything went wrong after that day.

60. Good advice

"Always turn the pillow." I think Virginia Woolf meant this to refer to a change of activity. But in these times, the domestic scientist Cheryl Mendelson and the life arranger Martha Stewart would mean just that: Turn the pillow. Or better yet, change the pillowslip, you filth packet. Never assume layers of meaning with an American. Go with the froth on the top.

Chicken today, feathers tomorrow.

Marry me. God, I was the wifey bargain of all time. I was a young, firm-feeling feminist who believed women should share the heavy lifting, loved small children while being emphatic that I would never bear children of my own, enjoyed housework and brought in an income. My parents were pleasant and lived far away. I loathed expensive wedding ceremonies, despised engagement rings, owned a sewing machine and knew how to line curtains, was fun at parties and hated vomiting so never made a mess. My knowledge of English literature was extensive and combined with an informed, though untrained, interest in architecture, Nixonian politics and the history of the postwar British Labour Party. Under stress, I would lose weight rather than gain it, but not on my breasts which were very large. I had travelled little and was rapturously grateful to be taken places like Virginia Woolf's house on my honeymoon. Raised in Kapuskasing, I knew nothing about exotic food and appreciated almost all cooked meals. I was happy to do the family bookkeeping and learn to garden, even the boring bits like correcting soil composition, and everything to do with Christmas, except for the making of a roast goose dinner, was done happily by me. Attracted to older men, I would make my husband's retirement a pensioned, still-incomed breeze.

If you didn't marry me, you should be kicking yourself right now.

61. Candy striper

I remember once driving past Calcutta's central hospital where plague had just broken out. How times have changed. For weren't hospitals once known as the place you were taken when you contracted the plague? It looked the type too, all stained concrete and hanging vines simultaneously rotting and growing metres by the hour. Germ soup. A sort of medical *bukkake,* that sexual practice where a gang of Japanese total bastards ejaculate simultaneously over some poor underpaid "actress." I wonder if she's allowed to get up and have a skin-scrubbing shower the minute the camera turns off or if she has to wait until she's completely stuck to the floor and the camera crew has to peel her off with letter openers and the paper cutters from their kids' origami project.

Canadian hospitals! Makes you think of the clean white crackle of the snow on Lake Louise. Is that Grey Goose, you ask, or just a special antiseptic for use in our pristine emergency rooms?

Actually, it's crusted pus and a whiff of excrement as I discovered after spending seven hours in a Toronto emergency room with a husband whose fingertip was clearly not going to be reattached—we would have had greater success with duct tape—and such being the case, wouldn't it have been nicer to dump his bed in the fetid corridor while the young woman screaming with the pain of endometriosis was prodded in a private room?

Ah, Alberta. Edmonton with its blue skies stretched as wide open as Paul Newman's morning smile fifty years ago. Alberta has a dry drunk for a premier but enough oil gushing out of the ground to pay for a health care system that might make my mother's angiogram, dare I say it, a tolerable experience. No, it was incompetently done, hell for my mother and awful for me to see.

In an angiogram, X-ray dye is pumped via an IV into an artery in the arm and the groin while they watch its path. As we were leaving, the nurse explained to me that my mother's wrist artery must not open up again. She then showed me precisely where it was on my arm (not where I had thought) and how to press it, and told me to call 911 if it began spouting blood.

This solved something that had troubled me about the story of Dr. David Kelly, the British scientist driven to suicide in 2003 by his own government after he disagreed with their assessment of Iraq's "weapons of mass destruction." He had five cuts on his wrist. Five? Wrist slitting is one of the toughest ways to kill yourself. You have to cut deep, and you must hit the ulnar artery, which isn't as easy as it sounds because, where is it, under your wristwatch? This complication has prevented many suicides.

So get this. The last thing the hospital tells me as we leave is the exact location of the crucial ulnar artery. In other words, here's how to off yourself.

That is truly funny. Peter Cook funny. (Cook was once found paralytic with laughter about a newspaper story that reported that corpses were being dug up from Frederick West's back yard. West's lawyer was complaining that "this kind of publicity might well damage his client's case.")

I didn't mention this bit to my mother because I would not have been able to keep a straight face.

Maybe they do this to everyone as they leave through the hospital's front door—here's some Seconal and a plastic bag, dear. Or perhaps you might just go on a cruise and jump overboard during the night. Mind that artery. Bye now!

62. Illnesses

I caught a cold and was perversely entertained by how awful it was—chest scratchy, exhaustion, the deep silent cold outside, piles of frozen brown slush on the roadway, the inconvenience of coats and bags and boots and scarves and gloves, the bare trees, the greyness, the horrors of urban January. If only you could go into a semi-slumber like bears, so it doesn't register as deeply. Really, turning into a puddle of fur and blubber for months on end would be Nature's sensible decree for us. But no. We must live through it, the price we pay for being the alert species that kills the happy hibernators. I might like a fur coat, but you need it more than I do.

63. At the fork of the body

Sex makes you more human. I have interviewed the ever helpful and amusing Stephen Fry several times on his book tours as he makes himself endlessly available to the press. He is always on time and immaculately courteous. Then came his collapse after a cruel review of the play *Cell Mates* in which he was appearing at the time. He fled to Bruges, of all places, and contemplated gassing himself in his car. He recovered. After sixteen years without having had sexual intercourse, he found himself a boyfriend. For the first time, he is late for the interview scheduled to discuss his second novel, *The Hippopotamus*. He finally appears, rumpled and yawning, and seems offended when I say I don't like the scene where the horse is raped after an application of "a bolus" of Vaseline jelly. I cannot see what it's doing in the book. (Later, when the first volume of his autobiography appears, he will reveal that he was raped at school by an older boy in just such a manner.) The spikier version of Fry is not as pleasant. But he's more human. Fiddling about with the tufted and smelly bits, as he would say, has made him normal.

Sex makes me languid. I'll sign anything, agree to holidays in Germany, drink liqueurs. I'm all stretchy and purring like a leopard.

I have always loved this sign of womanhood and was mortally offended once when a journalist introduced his commentary on a tampon advertisement with "I'm not squeamish but …." I would never disparage the bodily distinctions of men. Semen, for instance, smells fine, looks fine, tastes fine and even if it didn't, I wouldn't dream of mentioning it. But that's what our strange don't-ask-don't-tell attitude to periods does to me. I sound prissily polite.

I don't know who uses pads regularly rather than tampons, but a used pad has always struck me as an instant Rorschach in scarlet, a beautiful map. I miss them. Tampons are excessively convenient.

The German artist Kiki Smith has produced a sculpture called *Train,* in which a naked woman, a body cast made of white wax, is walking and looking over her shoulder as a stream of blood pours from between her legs. Only when you look closely do you see that they are four very long chains of red glass beads poured onto the floor. It is astonishingly beautiful. But given the way we are taught to see menstruation, she might also strike a viewer as a victim of a violent attack or as someone slightly shrunken in posture, as if she is ashamed of what is coming out of her.

Periods are a monthly gift, amazing in how promptly they arrive, sometimes to the actual hour. Cramps are terrible, endometriosis a tragedy, but a good menstrual cycle is something I find profoundly erotic. Why does no one ever talk about this? When Carly Simon got her first period, her mother took her up to the top balcony of the house and toasted the moon, and men. But even women who love being women turn all practical when it comes to periods.

I love buying menstrual products, even though they're hideously packaged and not even healthy with their emphatic chlorinated whiteness. There are pads, pantiliners in various colours and shapes (some with wraparound wings, some black which I don't like as the blood vanishes), menstrual cups, tampons in various sizes with cardboard inserters or ones where you just use your finger, despite the medicalized name "o.b." These products take up entire aisles in drugstores. When a woman visitor needs one of them, I start whipping out things. Thong? I say. Nighttime? Heavy-duty thins or the full diaper? Yes, I think this is funny. Especially when it's a subject generally dealt with as though it were infectious or temporarily dangerous, like a hot griddle pan that needs time to cool down. But it's this gorgeous blood flood! Red ink that promises an interior eroticism I shall one day miss. Discuss.

64. Presumptuous things

Pharmacists seeking to justify their dispensing fee comment on my prescriptions with frowns and much Tsking. Then they tell me

I will have to wait half an hour. Why, I ask. There are other patients ahead of you. Patients? "Lady, you count pills for a living" is what I want to say. I don't say it though. I know it would crush them like a pill. Funny that, as I don't mind being called a hack.

The director of the Harbourfront Reading Series in Toronto calls. Patricia Rozema, the director of *Mansfield Park,* has pulled out at the last minute for her onstage interview of Margaret Drabble. Can I fill in? You briefly wonder what the connection between *Mansfield Park* and Drabble's contemporary novels can possibly be. But you agree. The evening arrives. You sit with Drabble before going on and delicately feel your way, trying to find the words to ask her if you may bring up the subject of her suicide attempt when she was a young mother. You must have succeeded because she agrees. Onstage, she goes further. Her stomach was pumped and the doctors were rude, she recalls. How cruel, I say. No, I bloody deserved it, Drabble says cheerfully.

65. A young doctor at a clinic

A young doctor at a clinic is giving me a Pap test. A nurse stands by. It hurts like hell. I ask him to cover my legs with a sheet because it somehow seems less painful and distressing if you don't see how he's hurting you. He does so, knowing he should have done this before beginning. I complain of pain. He pulls the sheet back. This is the speculum that fits, he says, taking it out of me. See? Here's the bigger one. It won't fit. This is the right size. As if I'm buying a life jacket or a knife specifically for gutting pilchards.

Speaking of yokels, I remember another gynecological landmark. I am twenty. I am worried that I have an infection and go to an STD clinic at a Catholic hospital. Why? Because it's there and I don't know anything about religion. The patient preceding me is a Native Canadian woman, attractive in a brash way, a little coarse, a little fleshy. When I finally enter the examination room, an older man, the senior gynecologist, is saying with disgust, "We'll be seeing a lot of her." Also in attendance are a male intern and a middle-aged nurse, a slight woman who never says a word. They tell me to get up on the table. Without a gown? Just pull up your dress, they say. I have my period, I tell the nurse. Just put the tampon in the bin. It's a big round dark-green Rubbermaid garbage bin, the kind they now make in baby blue, with wheels on. So I pull up my dress, reach inside my panties and pull out the tampon, throwing it into the bin where it sits in a pile of unidentifiable stained things. The intern inserts his instrument. I tense, try to breathe slowly, clench my jaw, but eventually burst out, "What are you doing down there?" He is kind and apologizes profusely and tries again. The nurse says nothing.

The older man stands over me. He is wearing a fishing hat, like the one S. wears for gardening until I dispose of it immediately after writing this. It is decorated with fish hooks. Not corks or anything amusing, but actually hooked lures stuck into the hat. He takes over, does the test swiftly and painlessly as his hooks hang down with gravity over my spread legs.

I am supposed to see a nurse next, but I leave immediately. I never again allow a male gynecologist to touch me. I never again enter that hospital. Twenty years later, I protest when the hospital is merged with another hospital that does abortions and is given public funds. I have learned what many Catholic men think of disobedient, sexual women. They loathe us and enjoy inflicting what little suffering the government allows them to get away with. I despise them equally and rejoice as their religion wanes and becomes a relic in prosperous Western nations.

66. My long-time doctor leaves

My long-time family doctor leaves the city for the country, a case of abandonment as bad as that of any kitten tossed out of a moving car on the highway. I am stuck with one of those pale, lank-haired hippie doctors with a Women Who Run with the Wolves framed poster on her office wall and a coffee mug tree. Her clothes are shapeless. Worse, she gradually lures me out of medical treatment into some kind of psychology session, which I don't want. I just came for a flu shot, I want to wail. She looks like someone who's about to walk in front of a tram. What wolves does she run with, I wonder, the halt and lame, the ones with mange?

Really, she's a druggist, not a doctor, and suggests endless antidepressants (for me, not her, there's a puzzle). I tell her that I react badly to antidepressants, perhaps because I am not sufficiently depressed to need them. You must take the drug anyway, she says. This is not as bad as what I thought she was going to say which was "Boil a newt at midnight and score its liver with a hatpin." I leave her office and never come back. When she calls, I cravenly don't answer the phone. Where do you find these people? S. says disgustedly.

67. Enviable people

Martin Scorsese, who would wake up in the morning, write his former wife Isabella Rossellini, and say "Fuck it. Fuckitfuckitfuckit." Off to a fighting start.

The British TV critic Charlie Brooker, who wrote that he'd rather eat a big bowl of gravel and hair than sit through *Yentl* again. I moan and throw down the magazine. "I'll never write a phrase that clever." Yes, S. assures me tiredly, you will come up with many phrases that rival one about eating a bowl of gravel and hair.

I have lunch with the actress Shirley Douglas, mother of Kiefer Sutherland. She is in her seventies and has an elegant face, immaculate grey hair and the most beautiful mouth. It is like my thin-lipped mouth, which I have thought of as unfashionable, but on her it exemplifies the aimed-for perfection of another generation. Our desired lips are Julia Roberts puffy; theirs were slim Hepburn things. She wears red lipstick. It remains palpably red and perfect no matter what she eats. The woman could eat corn on the cob without disrupting her lipstick. Clearly, she does some disciplined actressy thing with her teeth that leaves her lips pristine. But what can it be? I praise her every time, which makes her laugh, so she is clearly doing it by instinct alone. Can it be taught? Mary Tyler Moore has confessed that her wide manic smile was born of her childhood terror of her dancing teacher. Did someone whack Shirley in the teeth with a metal ruler in 1942?

Anyone you see on the balcony of a great house along the Seine or Kensington Park or the Passeig de Gracia. They're likely rich, but they're definitely so distant that the agonies of their lives cannot be imagined. They're probably leaning on a balustrade pondering whether to jump. They probably envy me in my car. Some things look better just passing through, Elton John sings, and that's what I'm doing.

68. It's all in the phrasing

The chirpy style developed by newspaper medical reporters who want to sound upbeat. "Ditto the sputum analysis," they write gaily.

The phone company's Cash Management office: in French it translates as "Gestion de l'argent liquide." Please, may I work there? I imagine myself swimming in a silver lake, perhaps giving birth in it, to letter openers, picture frames and cuff bracelets.

69. Nothing annoys me so much

Nothing annoys me so much as movie stars who look like babies. Brad Pitt, Matt Damon, Leonardo diCaprio, Meg Ryan. Not only can I not tell them apart but I wince when they do adult things in their films. Look, you have a nose so puglike I can see up your nostrils. Your lips are so full of collagen they may well explode without warning. All the fat that was sucked out of your body has migrated to your cheeks. I don't think you should be pretending to have sexual intercourse in the movies you make together, I think you should be thrown on the bed and diapered. Meg Ryan, are you looking forward to sixth grade? Brad, do you open your squelching mouth at lunch and scream "Seafood!" at studio executives? Yes, I think he does that.

70. Features that I particularly like

A good jaw. Carly Simon has one. So does Sigourney Weaver, although I feel that a woman worthy of a jaw like that would not have felt the need to change her name from Susan Weaver.

The normal bodies of men. Exercised, toned male bodies, buffed and muscled, are repellent, especially those hard breasts like initially round packages that didn't survive postal handling, with those nipples that point downward. Imagine the work that went into that, when those men could have been reading or saying something clever, doing something with staying power.

71. Memories by scar

Thanks to my skin tone, and perhaps an emotional oversensitivity that expresses itself via the epidermis (well, you try and explain rosacea then), I scar badly from even the slightest injury. These scars last a minimum of six years. I can look at my limbs and spot a pizza oven burn, a lopper hack, an attack by a barberry shrub, a small circular scar from a dog's ringwormy lick twenty years ago, a cat scratch thirty-five years ago. I am obsessed by *Silent Witness,* a British crime show about forensic science. Would any of these humdrum scars help identify me? I don't go to dentists. Also, if I go missing and the police circulate a Last Seen Wearing, could I please be in something classy, something that doesn't sound like a bad day in Balham, nothing *shiny or clownish?*

72. Things that have lost their power

Everyone wants to be pretty, like Reese Witherspoon with blonde hair, a pink suit and perky expression and a steady flow of stupidity coming out of her mouth via a wire running down her back. But I have never wanted this. Pretty fades, pretty irritates. Short shelf life for pretty. I wanted to be interesting. I wanted to be strong. I wanted to be a person worth talking to after thirty. And if that meant dark hair and a face that worked but in no way anyone could explain, that was fine with me. And then my mother ruined it all by calling me Heather, the name of the classic pretty bitch. Reese's real name is Laura. My mother's name.

David Lean films

Movie musicals. Someone's standing with their legs slightly apart. They're looking at me. They're going to sing at me.

73. I have become bone-thin

I have become bone-thin, which is said to be wildly attractive but isn't really. Nicole Brown Simpson, that poor child who married a monster who carved her neck apart, used to judge her body on how she looked naked versus dressed. This had never occurred to me. I always assumed everyone thought of themselves as a constant, but she was living in PlasticSurgeryLand where people think differently. Anyway, I look good in good clothes, but really, I'm a bit ribby.

So during an attack of insomnia, I sit up to watch the sex channel, hoping I shall become a pheromone-emitting sex creature by inspiration. But the sex TV people have run out of things to say about the old in-out. The best they can offer is a documentary about personal hygiene among European porn performers.

A young German man says, subtitled, "I take a shower before and then I take a shower after. Then I take another shower before and I shower again. I shower about six times a day. It's a question of respect." They all use Wet Wipes. Wet Wipes, Wet Wipes, Wet Wipes. It's like a Swiffer channel populated by naked people. They keep their fingernails short. "It's a question of respect." And cuts, I imagine. Some of the younger actors have to be taken aside and talked to. "It's a question of respect." And Wet Wipes.

74. Why do moneyed women look better?

Why do moneyed women look better than the average woman? Surely their diet is reasonably similar and should produce clear skin in both. They both have worries, though not of the same kind. They both wash daily and go to hairdressers. The average woman can dress attractively on a normal budget; frequently a wealthy woman buys expensive strange clothes that don't flatter her. But the rich woman looks better. Are the ads right and it's all nothing more than sloshing moisturizer? If so, nearly every woman I know has wasted much of her life. It's all a question of butter, whether it's the stuff that comes out of shea nuts or the white strips on your bacon. Just mash it in your hands and lather it on.

75. Death mask

Death mask as beauty treatment in a spa: They steamed, cleansed, toned, exfoliated and hydrated my face. They pressed pads heavily into my eyeballs and placed a muslin cloth on my face with nose and mouth holes. Then they coated me with paraffin. What I felt like was the dead white-faced mother with coins on her eyes in the opening scene of *Dr. Zhivago,* being carried in her purple coffin to her burial hole, a mystery in the frozen steppes. No wonder the wind slapping branches against my windows last night terrified me. I could have been a stunned Yuri looking out the window for his mother and being consoled with a mandolin. They're playing Gregorian chants, which I try to drown out with a brain version of "Funeral for a Friend." Now's when I need a cell phone.

What I want to do is run screaming from the room, tearing the wax off my face and sucking in air. My nakedness prevents this.

76. Ah, beauty,

Will you be achieved if I stand here naked in a tiled room while a muscular, short-haired young woman sprays me with a high-pressure hose? For such is my situation. "This can't be too pleasant for Jews," I tell her, in a desperate attempt to normalize the situation by chatting. I am surprised when she says yes, she has had Jewish clients who became upset. Later, I am laid naked on an operating table, sanded and hosed down through nozzles in the ceiling. I am shattered. When I finally am given a bathrobe to cover my thin, reddened body, I look considerably less lovely than when I arrived at the spa. I look as if I've just been born—small, wrinkled, red and convulsed with panic.

77. Good advice that may or may not stick

"In many things one could not be superficial enough, she thought. And clothes could give one greater moral support than all appeals to justice, more than any amount of sympathy and understanding, more than all confessors, all wisdom, all perfidious friends, and even a lover. This was not frivolity; it was simply knowledge of the comfort and power that could lie in small things." This is from *Heaven Has No Favorites,* a novel by Erich Maria Remarque. May I just mention here that it was made into *Bobby Deerfield,* an Al Pacino movie I love but which sends my husband into hysterics and leads to much slamming of doors by me. Do I laugh at his favourite movie, *On the Waterfront*? (Yes, but later, by myself.)

A Slavic man speaks mournfully of the violence of Eastern Europe which appears to be chronic through the centuries. "You know why? We killed all the sensitive ones."

Monet's house at Giverny is beautiful, almost as beautiful as the gardens. But there is no denying that it is not lavish, only beautiful in a sensible, bourgeois kind of way. Luckily, that's my preferred way. The art of the paint chip and the blue and white cabinet for cooling eggs. Peace comes dropping slow.

I lose my temper in the gift shop they've created in Monet's studio. Why can't the French line up? Why do they allow doggery on the streets so that people regularly slip in it and break their legs? Why are American buttocks so big? Why are Canadians literal-minded? Why do Germans wear socks and sandals? Why can't New Yorkers grasp the concept of the stoplight?

Demi Moore's real name is Demetria Guynes. Yes, she was right to change it. But it was a bad move to build a million-dollar house for her doll collection. Give it to the servants. Only if they're very, very short, of course.

S. says my great tragedy is that I'm a stoic, but a sensitive one. He's an insensitive stoic and he does just fine.

Pour out my worries to my boss, telling him about every little staff problem eating at me. He laughs, says I'm being swarmed by gerbils.

78. Things without merit

No awards have merit. The judges are idiots. Look at who else won. You know this; nevertheless you accept their plaque, cheque and praise. Later at home, you punch yourself in the face for your hypocrisy.

The Nobel for literature went to whom? The guy who wrote *The Very Hungry Caterpillar*? That Scot, Irvine Welsh, who wrote summat about twats and keks and shite? Anyone but the great (and blacklisted) Doris Lessing, apparently.

We dine at the Oyster Bar under Grand Central Terminal in New York. Love the arches, the tiled ceilings, the affable service, the Sancerre, the hugeness of the room and the roar of conversation. We are very happy, our contentment dimmed only by the consistent awfulness of the food. How do you ruin a lovely piece of sole that never did a thing to you? And worse, where did you learn to serve it quickly and proudly? The portions are massive. I fill up on tea biscuits. Over and over, I notice this about big, beautiful U.S. restaurants. They're all show.

Kraft, the makers of Kraft Dinner, announces it will cut back on the fat content of its rubber foodishments. But I notice it hasn't said it will change its name to Craft.

Similarly, MasterCard now offers a wonderful new credit card called Mosaik, with different rules tailored to the individual needs of the customer. But the customer who badly needs her Mosaik card to be spelled correctly, as in Mosaic, is ignored. Or am I being unreasonable?

A bank machine gives me a $20 bill with a corner torn off, say, 15 percent of its acreage. When I attempt to use it, it is declined. So I go to the bank where I have been told it will be replaced instantly and with brio. Instead, there are endless consultations, little conferences with the manager. Where did you get this bill? Given that a wave of counterfeiting has led most stores to refuse $50s and $100s, which I am certain banks will not replace instantly and with brio, I feel cornered. Stores don't take legal tender. Now banks don't either. At least stores have milk, jade, drill bits and automobiles, all things I want. But banks? What are they for if they give my battered twenty the fisheye?

In Rome, I see a mannequin in a shop window wearing such garglingly ugly men's underpants that I take a photo of it. It's a black and grey pattern that looks like a snake with a bad rash. Then the posh clothing store where I buy most of my stuff comes up with a new store credit card. It's an American Express card, and I loathe Amex, partly for the same reason most stores do. It's a bully. But worse is the card itself. It's designed especially for us by Roberto Cavalli, they trumpet. And sure enough, there's the card, covered in those underpants.

79. Glaring things

You can tell right away if a novel's dreadful. Open it at random. If someone's looking up with a wry smile, a fire is crackling or a pool is sparkling invitingly, you're in for something putrid.

A woman next to me at a dinner tells me she is writing a mystery novel and is hoping to have it published. Have you read the latest Ruth Rendell, I say. It's one of her best. Who's Ruth Rendell? I explain and tell her she should buy it. Oh, I never buy books, the woman says. They're much too expensive.

A woman judging a fiction contest gushes over the Novel of the Year she has chosen. It's so good, I'm going to buy a copy, she says. And not just one. Several copies to lend to my friends. So a) she has no friends and b) she considers it astonishing to purchase a book. Is it as unusual as swallowing a small green snake? As using pomegranate seeds for earplugs? I mean, this is the judge, for god's sake.

80. Odd things

When talking to me about her father, one of my little stepdaughters would refer to him in his presence as The Man Who Sleeps Beside You. "I wish a man was moving in," the other one sighed when I appeared. On our wedding day, they gave us small dolls in wedding gear. The dolls were witty, wonderful sculpturettes made of stuffed pantyhose tied into shapes with features stuck on and hair made of ribbon. I was massive, a great big waddling thing in white. My husband was a tiny little creature tied to me. Their cards said: "You are stil my father even though you got maryed."

A woman friend, a mother of two who has endured much and looks permanently harassed, sends me a found-on-the-internet list of titles for children's books.

1. You Are Different and That's Bad
2. Dad's New Wife Robert
3. The Kids' Guide to Hitchhiking
4. Kathy Was So Bad Her Mom Stopped Loving Her
5. The Magic World Inside the Abandoned Refrigerator
6. Strangers Have the Best Candy
7. You Were an Accident
8. Things Rich Kids Have, But You Never Will
9. Pop! Goes the Hamster ... And Other Great Microwave Games
10. Your Nightmares Are Real
11. Why Can't Mr. Fork and Ms. Electrical Outlet Be Friends?
12. Daddy Drinks Because You Cry

The problem is, they're all useful and some are beautifully true, as William "useful and beautiful" Morris would have put it. I could have used some Morris-approved tales when I was a child.

I look at the summer fiction edition of an American magazine, boasting of its profusion of new short stories. Without exception, the Americans write about themselves, their high school, their city block and the house they grew up in. When bad things happen, like an advancing brain disease planted by both heredity and a virus, Americans always end up being grateful. Turning into a dribbler is an opportunity to live more deeply and richly, an inspiration to others. In other words, the story's canvas starts small and ends up tiny and perfect. All the action takes place in a city block and narrows down to the space between their ears, which in the case of the brain-disease man isn't that rewarding for the reader. But the other authors from Kabul, Calcutta, Lima, Russia and Japan write about bombings, train crashes, violent revolutions and lives so full of incident they spin like clothes in a dryer. The American would describe the clothes, the dryer, the lint trap. As Alan Bennett says, playing Trivial Pursuit with a life as constricted as his would be mere homeopathy. But even Bennett travels internationally. Furthermore, American writers rarely write about poverty. Or are those stories just not published? Is poverty considered too foreign?

I am tripped from behind and fall heavily onto the sidewalk, with no notion of what has happened to me. Only my hands, which are badly scraped, stopped me from falling on my face and smashing my teeth and facial bones. I can see the man's Kodiak boot inches from my face. "What happened? Did you faint?" he is asking. His voice sounds stretched and sinister, like a tape run slightly too slow. He moves on. People approach. That man did it, they tell me. We saw it happen. He attacked several other people before he got you.

Later, when I talk about it, everyone has a similar story. My brother-in-law was violently attacked on the street, as were the husbands of two of my friends. It was complicated by the fact that their attackers were all women, lunatics off their heads and off their medication. At least mine was a traditional mugging, I tell myself, where you recover as you watch your bloodied knees turn black and then yellow. I reacted to the man in the standard way, with shock. Whereas the rest of them all felt they could hardly punch a woman in the face. I would have loved to have done so, but lack the nous, the fist, the ability.

81. Squalid things

Most men are new to intensive personal grooming, which one would think would have given them extra cash and free time and contributed to their entirely unjustified sense of being without flaw. But now they are flailing. A fat man in a bathrobe sits atop a banquette in an expensive spa, having a pedicure. He sprawls as if he were on the subway taking up two seats. He is wearing baby blue Jockey underpants. His genitals bulge between his round thighs, like a baby's. I am at eye level and I lock my legs together to hide my own naked crotch. His wife sits next to him with her legs together, as her own feet are sanded by a crouched and beautiful young woman. The double pedicure was her Christmas gift to him and she knows the drill. But why does she not tell him? She wants him to look better, perhaps not scrape her in bed. But she won't tell him how not to make a fool of himself in a spa. This is a sign of her hate.

A woman leaves a bathroom cubicle at a bar and washes one finger.

I read of how Lee Radziwill, a daft and pretentious woman morally worth not a fraction of her famous sister, gave a party and decreed that the toilet must always be graced with a fresh gardenia. Her Filipina maid spent the evening pushing in front of waiting guests and tossing gardenias in a toilet that had just been flushed, gardenias that would then be immediately fouled by guests who rather liked gardenias and would be repelled by the sight of their leavings on the innocent flower with scents blended. I hope someone got a poem out of this party in 1966.

On the other hand, I don't wish to come within a mile of the peelings of a whale testicle whether they cover the barstools of Aristotle Onassis's yacht or not.

82. Bad advice

A woman with a personality disorder that isn't borderline advises me to "flirt shamelessly" with my boss. She herself has the contours of an unbaked muffin, the kind that you poke and the batter doesn't spring back. She is iced with psychosis. But what the hell, I'm in his office and he praises my work so I feel flirting is pointless and therefore won't violate my principles. I toss my hair alluringly. No notice is taken. I do it again. "Why are you doing that? Are you all right? Is there something wrong with your neck?" He sleeps on a special pillow for his neck, he tells me.

83. Shameful things

When people you admired accept a seat in the House of Lords. When slimy people you know to be cowards win the Order of Canada. When the U.S. Senate votes unanimously.

You watch the real estate channel in Buffalo on Sunday mornings, mesmerized by hideous (but fantastically cheap) bungalow after hideous A-frame. There is one thing you never see and never will see in these homes: a bookshelf. You are satisfactorily sickened by this until you think of your own bookless neighbourhood and how it is second nature to you never to mention reading material. Some people might read the neighbourhood paper for the real estate ads. Few people read the city newspaper. But no one reads books or magazines. And it isn't to be discussed. You'd sooner ask if people preferred to spit their gobs or swallow them than refer to a book.

84. Annoying things

It isn't the reading glasses I mind in my forties. It's the magnifying glass I use to read the instructions on my MP3 player that makes me cringe. I suppose this is a variant on the fact that only old people have enough money to go on cruises, thus I never go on cruises as I don't like hanging around a boat full of old people. I can afford an MP3 player but really, it's for the young. They should make the little map of the MP3 player buttons much bigger, but they won't because they don't cater to irritated over-forties with money to burn on pointless gadgets.

I call my local councillor because the garbage has been sitting uncollected on the streets of our neighbourhood for four days. Not only does her phone go unanswered but I get a lengthy message listing the matters she will not deal with and does not wish to hear about: garbage, stray animals, city works, in fact, all the dull things a councillor is paid to deal with but feels are beneath her. I imagine my own message: I do not wish to hear about: Hollywood, religion of any kind, what wine tastes like, how big the cyst was, jazz or its history … look, it would never end.

The garrulous woman who lives in the street behind us has a voice like a hacksaw. She's one of those people who slides the knife in and out as she chats with you, something Helen Fielding's Bridget Jones likens to a jellyfish sting. I tell her I work for a tabloid. She would never buy that paper, she says, and changes the subject. Now that I work for a posher paper, it is never mentioned. She says "We didn't think your new roof matched the house at all. But now that we look at it, we think it works." I had regretted my choice of shingle but shook the feeling off. Now thanks to her, I have a good decade of roof-doubting ahead of me. Everyone else has a beige house. But the oddness of not-beige repels her and she doesn't have the courtesy to hide it. I feel like painting my entire house the colour of Kristin Scott Thomas's nipples, just to fix her bacon.

And then I remember that, like most of us, Ms. Scott Thomas has beige nipples.

On any trip, you will always forget one crucial item. You will have forgotten the children's underwear and, insane with jet lag, be forced to stock up in Marks & Sparks on Oxford Street during the Gay Pride parade on the hottest day of the year. You will scour Moscow for tampons, San Diego for books, Paris for a watch battery and a clock that glows in the dark, Calcutta for liquor (and Glasgow for liquor too, which is puzzling). On the flight out, try guessing. But I swear, it will not occur to you until you've disembarked.

85. Oh the sadness

People who are thrilled to win Employee of the Month TAB awards. What does TAB stand for? Thanks a bunch! No, there's no cash with that.

The actor Rob Brydon in the British TV series *Human Remains* plays the gentle, bullied, unloved husband of a deeply unpleasant woman with full-body vaginismus who goes into the garden and

French-kisses the letters carved into her dead boyfriend's tombstone whenever she gets drunk. The pseudo-documentary camera turns to him. Does he think he has been dealt a bad hand in life, the unseen reporter asks.

He answers, half-man, half-moron, sitting on a child's swing. "Friends ... and not even friends, but acquaintances ... have said, 'Life has dealt you a bad hand.' Well, I'm pretty philosophical about that. If a life of turmoil ... anguish ... sorrow ... doubt ... fear ... regret ... and longing is a bad hand, then yes, I've been dealt a bad hand."

Pause.

"But is it?"

"But is it?" has become the sarcastic shorthand in our house for every ludicrous misfortune.

86. Things that are rarely seen

I am working on a newspaper story about a local abortion clinic and am invited in to watch abortions take place. At the patient's request, she is shown what has been extracted. There's no fetus, of course, despite the anti-abortion propaganda, not even anything that can be identified, just some uterine linings. It looks as though she had a period in three minutes rather than five days. The relief of the young girl is enormously affecting. I think she had been expecting a very small baby.

As I am leaving, a young woman accompanied by her mother arrives for an abortion. They are from the same small town I came from, and the counsellor mentions my name. The mother tells the counsellor that my father delivered her daughter, that very girl. My father is dead, as dead as possible, his ashes poured into a lake. But this girl is here, free and able to make her choice, helped by doctors. It's as if a ghost has spoken to me.

I once spotted a letter behind the phone at my parents' house. It was that small-sized stationery edged with a floral pattern that I would never buy, but that mothers buy. It was a thank you letter from a woman whose daughter's life was saved by my father. He was driving along and passed a wreck on the highway (like that Springsteen song whose tune is "Green Green Grass of Home"; explain that theft, Bruce). Out of the corner of his eye, he thought he saw something move. And he stopped and he had. He treated the young woman in the wreck and made sure she had a backboard when the ambulance came lest some missed spinal injury become paralysis. What puzzles me is that I had to extract this story from my mother at the time. No fuss was made. Like Woodrow Call in Larry McMurtry's great Western novel *Lonesome Dove,* we were not a family of mentioners. We were not Gus McCraes, as you'll understand if you read the book, which you should.

Babies on their backs like to fling out their arms and clutch the air. Perhaps this becomes unnerving. They may then pull their arms in and curl their thumbs into their palms. I'm sad that the most trustworthy thing available is their own thumbs but it will do. And then I see the death photos of Nicole Brown Simpson, released quite rightly by her family, who wanted the world to know what Orenthal Simpson was going to get away with. Sure enough, her head almost hacked off, her black dress soaked in blood and her face still perfect and beautiful, her bloodied hands are curled in on themselves, clutching their thumbs. Please let this have given her some comfort as it all ebbed away.

87. Things you thought were long gone

A prominent woman will be introducing *Harper's* editor Lewis Lapham at a luncheon where he will give a speech. The last time you saw her, you were with your husband. She embraced you warmly and kissed you. This time you are alone. You smile as you approach her to say hello. But without a man beside me, she doesn't know me. I simply do not register.

88. Speaking of Henry

I am having lunch with Dr. Henry Morgentaler, now eighty, who faced down the Nazis and specifically the Mengele monster eye-to-eye on the train platform at Auschwitz, and later the assembled legal and police force of the Canadian federal and provincial governments when he fought for—and won—abortion rights for women. I always feel not quite up to these lunches. Henry makes me think of the line from Joseph Conrad's *Lord Jim* on "how to be," as this was a question Henry struggled with for decades. Stein tells Jim, "A man that is born falls into a dream like a man who falls into the sea. If he tries to climb out into the air as inexperienced people endeavour to do, he drowns—nicht wahr? ... No! I tell you! The way is to the destructive element submit yourself, and with the exertions of your hands and feet in the water make the deep, deep sea keep you up."

Henry was first plunged into the destructive element as a boy. But the second time was by choice. He exited a comfortable doctorly life and went off to prod the huge greasy lizards of government again. How it would have enraged the Nazis to see him win, to get his way, to laugh in their faces one more time. And he has mastered smaller catastrophes, like divorces, loss of custody of a much-loved child, depression and illness, which bring the rest of us to our knees.

Compared to Henry, I have mastered very few catastrophes. Francis Bacon, deploring modern artists, said they want painless achievement, "the grin without the cat, the sensation of life without the boredom of conveyance." I suspect this is me, sitting across from Henry and sharing his knowledge of pain vicariously without having suffered its conveyance. I feel shame.

Some way, somehow, Mengele's name comes up. He drowned in the surf in 1979, I tell Henry, who expresses surprise (but he must have known, surely) and says quietly that that was too quick a death for that man. Later, I read and discover that Mengele's life post–Third Reich was a misery. He fled to South America and moved from country to country working at menial jobs on farms, afraid to go out at night and always afraid that Mossad was on his tail, which it was. He had to marry his sister-in-law, the marriage market for mass serial killers and torturers of children being strictly limited even in Nazi circles. And the death wasn't quick. Mengele's landlady urged him to go outside in daylight, get some sunshine. He went to the beach. While swimming, he had a stroke, and drowned. I want to tell Henry this, ask Henry about the pain of his own minor stroke, tell him to imagine Mengele's terror and his unheard cries for help, his wild splashes while happy children shrieked with pleasure in the water, his realization that he would die ignominiously, all alone, without a helping hand. Not waving but drowning.

But as I offer all this, Henry shakes his head each time. No suffering was extreme enough for Mengele. I curse myself for my stupidity in even bringing up the subject. Henry triumphed over Mengele in a hundred ways, one of them by being the kind of man who won't sneer at young women, who laughs at life, who will say when someone gets tight-assed, "Why shouldn't my patient have thirteen abortions? Does she sound like she wants to be a mother? She's making the right decision every time."

I'm seeing him tomorrow. I'll apologize. I'll give him *Lonesome Dove.* Henry's a mentioner and a noticer. Women like mentioners and noticers. Henry would much prefer that I drink a shot of vodka and shout with laughter and be indiscreet. He ordered me my first shot in a Montreal restaurant where I also had my first blini, my first borscht, my first caviar. Enjoy life, Henry says. The vodka tells me to flip away the fretting. The vodka's right. He's right. But how did Henry learn to shake off his pain, if indeed he has, after the worst century in the history of mankind? How does he know what he knows?

89. A letter writer

A letter writer tells me about American warriors. He had just got out of the Canadian Army himself in the early 70s. He ran into some U.S. Marines and, for once, felt able to bring up the subject of Vietnam. What was it like over there? he asked one man.

"He did not speak right away. For a few seconds I really thought I had hit the wrong button. Then he spoke. 'It was like a bunch of people going camping and nobody had ever gone camping before.'"

90. Nothing entertains me so much

Nothing entertains me so much as hearing people tell me that they can't read the novels of Margaret Atwood, can't stand the stuff.

Ooooh, her books are so gloomy, and her characters aren't nice, they say, the implication being that they themselves are very nice and the sun always has its hat off for them. But it's a marker. I can never quite trust anyone who says this. No, change that. The remark is merely a silly one, but its effect on me is more dire. It's like a red slash on a hog, a mark for slaughter. I feel a sadistic desire to stuff that candy bar down their throats. Open your eyes, I want to say. See your world, just for once, as it really is. Let Atwood read your palm. Read *Oryx and Crake* and tremble.

91. Atwood herself

Atwood herself is heavenly. I was working for a woman-hating tabloid and was granted an hour with her to talk about *Alias Grace,* perhaps because these were readers she would not normally reach. Atwood told me with amusement and some sympathy that I was like the fiction editor of *Playboy* magazine, holder of a truly thankless job. You can't have it both ways, she said. "Of course I can," I said. "Why can't I?" I was young and it had never occurred to me I couldn't have anything both ways. Her assistant came over tapping her watch. Atwood caught the look of horror on my face—we've hardly started, it pleaded—and gave me another hour.

She is reputed to be so tough. Yet when she entered a huge room of bookish people that night, she looked apprehensive, almost frightened. She was the queen, she was the smartest girl in the class, but they always make you pay in blood for that. I hailed her happily and walked over to shake her hand. Her face changed instantly. She was so relieved to have an ally to greet her until her phalanx could join her. I was touched, and concerned.

A literary agent, a lacquered woman with helmet hair and a pink suit, came over and grilled me about how I knew Atwood. I don't, I said. I was just saying hello. I see, the woman said dismissively, and walked away.

92. Adorable things

The bellies of little girls, which they puff out proudly. Their bodies are all curves, all S-shapes.

My girlfriend's little boys haul me downstairs shouting in starter English I can just barely understand. Apparently a giant bug has crawled into the playroom and the lady Heather must kill it. Little do they know that the lady's liver quivers at the sight of millipedes. Hmmm, can't see it, I say, playing for time. Mum comes home and mashes the thing across the rug which I think is NOT the way to kill lengthy bugs thick with legs but who am I to complain? I bask in reflected glory.

93. Unsuitable things

Middle-aged women with cruel hair, those harshly dyed razor-cut wedges that are practical if nothing else. The female version of the mullet with the lower half shaved off.

The cartoonish fat of A.S. Byatt's face, like a pug, combined with her pepperpot body and fondness for hats, makes her attacks on beauty and youth and humour and anything popular seem repulsive, as if they were a sort of revenge. I always feel an urge to stick a two-pronged fork into her nostrils.

I am watching a nature documentary in my parents' home. I am in university by now. What could be more anodyne, less likely to cause difficulty with my mother, than watching a documentary on whales? And then the whale's giant erection flings itself out of the water. It must be two storeys high. It's pink and purple in places. It trolls through the water like a giant's finger. I am frozen in embarrassment, as we are a family that never mentioned, much less discussed, sex. Even in animals. And David Attenborough or whoever is droning on about the male whale member and I'm silently ranting "Get on with it you stupid lardy show-offy pervert, no wonder they call them animals." Humans are surely the only mammals where the female gets on top sometimes, so the male must do all his humping with his member underwater. But no, it looks like he has to air-dry it or something while Attenborough chunters on. They couldn't have spent more than five minutes on the thing but it felt like an hour, this giant purple cock like the periscope of a huge submarine parading across the TV screen as we (or perhaps just I?) sat in horrified silence.

The same thing happens years later when my mother is visiting and I put on a suitable video for her, John Cleese's *A Fish Called Wanda*. What could be more harmless? And I see it through my mother's eyes. It's filth, filth, I tell you. Breasts and willies and things. Should have got her *Planes, Trains and Automobiles,* I think. Last week, I watched that one on actual TV and to my disappointment they had taken the word "fucking" out of Steve Martin's rant to the bubble-brained car lady who sent him to an empty space where a rental car should have been. The humour is non-existent in the "propered" movie. It is impossible to win with one's mother. It's not like with little kids and sexual references. My mum gets it.

94. Surprising and distressing things

That children should be mocked at school for poverty. We adults devise our own tortures for the failures, but children's arise spontaneously, and so early.

The man who mends my shoes with great skill is telling me that he took his children to the dentist. The dentist took him aside and said "When did you last bring them in?" Two years ago, he answered. "That's not good enough," the dentist said.

But I don't have the money, the man told me. And I know what he means. Why don't they raise my taxes so this man can have his children's teeth cleaned and mended? I would happily pay. And once again, I wonder about why teeth are not covered by public health insurance, why they are considered an unusual event in the body. They're bones after all but on the outside. And eyes? Why are yearly eye tests not paid for by the government? We punish children via teeth and eyes. If it isn't coated with skin, it isn't covered, literally.

95. Things that give a hot feeling

You are dressed for dinner in Paris in a way that you know will entirely meet with the satisfaction of the proprietor and the waiters. It requires expense and effort. You are perfect. But the intelligent part of you, which appears to be shrinking by the minute, knows the whole charade is complete nonsense.

You speak at a party to a man who you know once broke his wife's jaw. Normally, you would not even attend a party where someone like this has been invited. He is short, portly, and has lank yellow hair. He then says a number of things that you know full well to be lies and that he would know, if he had any understanding of human relations, would be obvious to you as whoppers. Instead of being outraged, you watch his eyes and mouth, looking for clues, fascinated. I'm listening to Theodore Bundy saying he didn't kill those women. I'm listening to Colin Thatcher saying he didn't bludgeon his beautiful wife to death in her garage. I'm watching a psychopath casually map his past. There's no doubt here. They are lies built like alphabet blocks; they don't even bother to make themselves difficult to fit together. Watch, I tell myself. Learn. But I discover nothing. If I didn't know they were lies before, I doubt I'd spot them now. This is a terrible thing to learn about your imperceptions. I hope homicide cops do better than this.

96. The best compliment ever

I walk down the locker-lined hallway in high school and make a passing casual arrangement to see friends that night. My friend Liz Clarkson, who is an exchange student from Australia, says she is stunned by my social ease. But Liz, I want to say, I live here. You're in a foreign country. Furthermore, I was talking to my best friends. It's all an illusion. I never accept compliments and always correct anyone who has a favourable—and, by definition, wrong—impression of me. One sees how easy it is for people like

Liz to rate themselves unfavourably for reasons that are utterly specious. (Nevertheless, it was a bloody good compliment and warms me in my lean years.)

I take a *Sunday Times of London* survey on my literacy—my book IQ, my love of language and ability to grasp it quickly, the quickness of my mind as it relates to words. To my amazement, I score at the absolute top level. They say they have no words to describe my abilities, which are so extensive it gives them the collywobbles. I am "difficult to categorize."

Difficult to categorize? Heather "Difficult to Categorize" Mallick. It's a better middle name than Linda; perhaps I shall change it. I am floating a foot off the sidewalk for years. I still boast of it. I'm boasting now. For once, I will accept the justice of a compliment, sort of maybe. Mummy, I'm difficult to categorize!

97. This passing parade

This passing parade took place on a greasy grey windy day that only cities in February can produce. I wanted to fill my brain with the background chatter of a busy restaurant, drink Bloody Caesars and laugh with a friend.

When we get there, we are the only customers in the place. We sit in front of a huge plate-glass window. My companion is plump and her errant bra straps travel, cutting into her flesh. It seems to symbolize the discomfort of the day. Our drinks are bland and she sends them both back for Worcestershire and/or Tabasco. Feeling sorry for the bartender who is clearly on his first day, I say to the waiter, "I hope the bartender isn't offended." "I made them," he says. What does spit taste like, I wonder.

We stare out the window where a German shepherd trots by in little red knitted boots, which imply there is an owner somewhere. The dog squats in front of us and lavishly expels an impressive amount of pale brown diarrhea. He trots off.

This was a defining moment. What kind of person are you? Are you the kind who sits there giggling as men and women tread—splat!—in the diarrhea? Or are you the kind who gives up on the meal, plays Lancelot and repeatedly bangs on the plate glass to alert passersby to the mess? Let's up the ante. When an Italian wedding party climbs out of a rented tour bus to be photographed in front of the restaurant—presumably this restaurant is where they met or meaningfully opened small velvet boxes—do you alert the bride who looks tearful and stressed-out already (this day is the highlight of her life because she is Italian) to the stinking spreading spill that is about to travel along her white silk hem?

I alerted the bride. My friend just laughed. Then my friend began bouncing in her seat, having seen Margaret Atwood and her daughter Jess Atwood Gibson walking along arm-in-arm. She adores spotting celebrities—seeing them makes her briefly part of their life, which improves on her middle-class childhood—and is praying that Atwood steps in the shit.

She does not. She strides past, nowhere near the excrement. The woman who wrote *Bluebeard's Egg* and *The Handmaid's Tale* is hardly going to make a misstep. Inside, I am cheering.

98. I am at a party (Jelly Belly)

I am at a party I should have known better than to attend. Rough people. People from work and other works. An older obese dyed-blonde woman whom I have known and disliked for two years at work comes into the kitchen where everyone is crowded because they have to be somewhere and why not the kitchen. My back is turned to her. Behind me, she edges past. Then she bends over and dry-humps me on the corner of the kitchen table. I can feel a lump? a mound? grinding into my ass, and breasts that feel floppy and jelly-like against my shoulder blades. I can smell her. She feels amorphous yet still crushing, like a walrus. She's an alcoholic, I know, but maybe the lesbian aggression only comes out once a year? I will never forget the glucose breast sensation. Since I have no idea what other women's breasts are supposed to feel like, I ask men. They say jelly isn't normal, but if they were fake, wouldn't they be big? So perhaps they're just old fat milk glands. S. tactfully says he can't remember other women's breasts. How I envy him. I'll never forget this pair.

99. Enemies List

The chief of police (whom I always refer to as the "piece of chaleef," from an obscure joke in a really rather good 1970s show called *Soap*) says Toronto has a list of 400 Most Wanted Criminals. For this he was roundly mocked, in that the FBI list only runs to 10, and the Royal Canadian Mounted Police, hysterics all, are hunting down 28. Even Richard Nixon's enemies list only came to 218.

And there I was, laughing, until I realized that my own list would be closer to the length of the chief's than it would of Nixon's. This can't be good.

Rude waitress in an Edinburgh restaurant, after dispute over egg salad sandwich, 1974.

Landscaper who greeted my complaint that he hadn't mixed the peat moss/topsoil/compost, thus killing my azaleas, with "Lady, it's just a bunch of dirt," 2003.

Huge hulking Prince William, who is said to have killed a fourteen-inch-tall dik-dik with a spear. Dik-diks are little furry muffins the size of babies, toddlers tops. How Princess Diana would have suffered upon hearing she had given birth to the inevitable sadistic royal oik. 'Twas all for naught, 2003.

Shoe salesman who fondled me after Keds purchased, 1993.

Those who installed almost everything in my home: carpeting, drywall, tile flooring, light fixtures, deck, insulation, showers, toilets, sinks (I see that bathrooms are a particular trouble spot for plumbers).

Montauk, for making ludicrously big sofas that increase urban sprawl. I swear, they build bigger houses just to accommodate them.

Nicolas Cage, for gawping.

Bruce Willis, for smirking.

Ralph Fiennes, for having that huge lump in his forehead. I understand a brooding presence is a must-have for actors who can't cope with dialogue, but shouldn't he have it looked at?

People who drop me off, saying, "Gee, you have a cute house." It's not cute. It's dark green and perfectly sensible. It keeps out leaks. What am I, Mother Hubbard?

The skunk/raccoon/fox/marmoset/Hoon that used the same six square inches of sedum in my rock garden as his toilet each night. You just know he's thinking, "She's too nice to poison me. I bet she likes cats." I don't like cats that much.

100. People who play up to their reputation

David Hockney is marching through London with the Countryside Alliance, not in favour of fox hunting per se but because he's a libertarian. His placard reads "End Bossiness Now." But it seems too abrupt, even un-British. So he changes his slogan to "End Bossiness Soon."

Alan Bennett writes a short story sympathetic to a pedophilic character just out of prison who gets a maintenance job in the public gardens and attacks a little girl, a flirtatious little girl, as he and Bennett would put it. Is there anyone Bennett doesn't like? I suspect he saw something nasty in the woodshed when he was a child, and as he writes in *The London Review of Books* many years later, he did. In real life, the man's pursuit of little Alan was terrifying, at least to the reader. Bennett's fictional response is mystifying. Is this what they mean by the Dunkirk spirit, the boy managing to escape in his little boat while French Jewish children perished?

Auberon Waugh plays down his frequent childhood experience of being whipped with a cane on his naked buttocks by a teacher who is sexually aroused by the evident pain. "I cannot find it in my heart to grudge him such little consolations," he writes. He feels he must be British about it, but he simply seems insane.

On the other hand, Waugh writes that his mother might have been happier if she'd married someone other than his father. "But I am not really all that sure how happy anyone's life is, when one comes to examine it." His claim that being tortured as a child never affected him must be untrue. I'll speak bollocks here, he must think, as readers expect it of me.

101. People I admire

The American playwright and essayist Jean Kerr who died in 2002 of old age was in the S.J. Perelman class. She was one of the funniest women in print, but like Erma Bombeck who wrote brilliantly about family life, she never got the credit she deserved. She once wrote of the woman *she* most admired, a woman she overheard saying gently to her little boy on a hot day "Mummy doesn't *like* you to ride your bike into the piano." I took her point. That would have been the woman I most admired too.

102. People who suffer

Years ago I read this, somewhere long forgotten: "I heard a man say to an inquisitive woman at a dinner party in London: 'Please don't ask,' he said softly. 'I don't have anything interesting to tell you. I've made a terrible mess of my life.' Six months later, he killed himself."

It's the "softly" that drives it.

Leonard Woolf says in his diaries that he doesn't believe in being happy. But do I really have to give up my artful scheme of happiness just because the monkish Leonard says so? Do I really have to forget that flood of delight, Clarissa Dalloway–like, when I stood on Oxford Street perfectly alone in a foreign city and said "No one knows me here"? And that moment of exhilaration in that pub behind Liberty, that private moment of unjustified elation that struck without warning. And when I marched down the alley of trees in Kew towards the pagoda, never had I felt such expansion in my heart. But Leonard Woolf says no.

103. Things that one is in a hurry to see or hear

The Junior Bush era over. But this killer vine, now planted, will snake on forever.

The current head of the U.S. Environmental Protection Agency, whose job it is to cover his eyes while they pour lead slurry into the Grand Canyon, come down with a touch of asbestosis, which he would say chirpily is handy in a house fire. Republicans like to see the bright side of man-made illness, but they've banned class action lawsuits, just in case.

104. Things at which one shouldn't laugh but does anyway

Watching a BBCWorld news report on the tarting up of St. Petersburg for its 300th anniversary. An old woman in an apartment building near the Winter Palace complains that the city is painting its grand buildings but doing nothing about her crumbling flat. She removes layers of rugs to reveal a rotting floor through which she may well fall. Her husband has already been injured; he was taking a bath and the whole thing went through the floor. By coincidence, both these things happened with bells on in *The Money Pit,* that 1986 Tom Hanks movie about a disastrous renovation. I still watch it once a year and laugh myself sick. I want to ask the old woman if she has done a Shelley Long and run screaming through the hallways with a dumbwaiter-inhabiting raccoon attached to her face. When the floor literally swallows her, will she be bagged halfway by an Oriental rug and lose her mind as she dangles between floors, spending the night singing to herself? And does she have weak trees?

The Lloyds Bank Turd was discovered in 1972 and lies in the York museum in the north of England. Named after the site of its excavation, it's twelve hundred years old and is the largest fossilized human excrement ever found. Dumped by a Viking, its content—meat, bran, fruit stones and worm eggs—is less interesting than its size. It's huge. The museum regularly gets letters from schoolkids. "Thank you for showing us the poo," they read. This year, a teacher showing the thing in its display case to a class of hooting children made the news by dropping it and breaking it into three pieces. I want this teacher's name. For not only do the British papers run pictures of the great big thing with a pointed end, they go wild on headlines. *The Guardian*'s is the best: "Museum's broken treasure not just any old shit." I laugh for days, to my S.'s mystification. He had thought he'd married a bit of posh, only to discover she's a bit of rough who goes into hysterics at toilet jokes.

The British author Mil Millington used to run a website, part of whose raison d'être was to invite readers to nominate the worst loo they had ever encountered on vacation. My favourite was the one where a couple saw a drunk go into a Portaloo in the middle of the night, stagger about and knock the thing over. Apparently Portaloos disgorge their contents when horizontal, which is bad enough, but the killer was that the Portaloo had fallen *with the door side down.* The best part was the crowd that gathered. Who was going to do the decent thing? Finally, two saints uprighted the plastic coffin and watched something horrible and stinky and tragic emerge.

Millington was forced to remove the website from his employer's server, which he did, closing with a plaintive question about whether it was, as his self-righteous colleagues claimed, the most offensive thing they'd ever read. And people from all over the world, including me, emailed back saying, god no, it's hysterical. I adore Millington, my great literary companion whenever I get depressed about the state of the world. As the fragile and wonderful memoirist Anne Lamott would say, you need writers like this in your pit crew.

105. Things you never expected to have to do

You wash your own sheets weekly. But somewhere in your brain, you have to keep a running total of the number of times S. has been exiled to the spare bedroom after a dispute that at the time seemed worthy after the bottle of Côtes du Rhône was drained, i.e., Could Lee Marvin act? or Don't you ever bloody like *anything*? At seven nights, the bed must be stripped for laundry. You lie awake at night feeling ashamed as you calculate. That it's come to this, you think. The power and the glory.

Under great stress, you forget your birth control pill five days running. You are forty-four years old and have never missed it for more than a day or two. Your doctor has warned you about this sort of complacency. There are two kinds of women who get pregnant, she tells me: fertile women, and women like you who think they don't have to bother any more, what are the odds ha ha.

And for the first time, you honestly wonder if you will have to go to a clinic, have laminaria inserted in your cervix and get scraped out. Your determination never to have children has always been diamond-hard. And now you'll be the oldest lady in Henry's waiting room. Maybe you can pass yourself off as someone's auntie.

When the blood arrives, you thank The Good Body and whatever goddesses there may be.

106. Things that are pleasant

The transsexual Jan Morris was a peculiar child, no surprises there, but even then and through his life, he was always striking up conversations with strangers. He thought of it as his ticket to a club of which he later must have realized he would never be a member, i.e., normal people. I do this too and take great pleasure in it, talking to anyone about anything, in airports, in stores, in the seat next to me. People approach me all the time and we blather away. S. is fascinated, but secretly appalled. Men don't do this.

107. The shadow of things that are pleasant

James Morris, the mountaineer, was an extraordinarily handsome man. As the woman travel writer, he was a mess, a hag really. His excuse for chatting to strangers was that he thought it was a womanly thing to do. But had he ever chatted to me, I'd have responded out of sympathy, not interest. Why is it that transsexuals always choose to become the sex in which they are less attractive, where they don't have a shred of hope?

108. Actressy things

Emma Thompson says her marriage (to Kenneth Branagh) has "earthed" her. "One of the most attractive male qualities is the capacity to earth a volatile woman." She and Branagh are now divorced.

Miranda Richardson says she fell ill for two years after her first film success. How nice for her. The rest of us don't have two income-free years to rest up from our wonderful experiences. Or even our appalling ones.

I am entranced by a beautiful gown designed by Olivier Theskeyns, the Belgian designer. The cream silks fall perfectly from the shoulders to the waist where they form a huge skirt sliced open at the front. The underskirt is fur, from waist to ankle. I love it, I tell S. It's the most beautiful, sexual dress I have ever laid eyes on. He is unmoved. "You do realize the fur is intended to suggest pubic hair, and 'suggest' is the kindest word I can think of." Oh.

109. Small things that took years to learn

In a Paris restaurant named Baracane, I see through a pass-through gap in the kitchen door the hands of a man peeling pears, dozens of them. He does it in one unrolling strip, never pausing, never making an error.

In journalism class, one is taught never to begin a story about a public survey with "Broken down by sex, poll respondents ..." It sounds obvious but apparently it's not.

110. Obsessive compulsion

Weeding. Each weed requires a different approach. But the dandelions on my friend's farm demand deep penetration, something like those Bangalores they had on the Normandy beaches. Their single thick roots reach six inches down. They cannot be teased out like a carrot. The entire surrounding area must be laboriously excavated like the earth around a Roman chariot inconveniently discovered while building a highway, or that brown hairy rod will grow again. I'm against Killex. This time it's personal. That weekend, I figure I gathered twenty pounds of landscape disfigurement. It's like bomb disposal. I learn that I need the Jekyll weeding fork but it will cost thirty-five pounds sterling plus duty, imported from England. Learn to love dandelions. Think of them as tulips with Struwelpetter hair.

Painting. I hired two women to paint my grotty bathroom walls gleaming white, paste a broad border of Beatrix Potter Goes to the Seaside along the top and paint the ceiling a pale turquoise blue. This and the yellow sand of the border looked like the beach at St. Ives looking out to the lighthouse that inspired Virginia Woolf, which is quite something for a bathroom. Of course, St. Ives was nothing like this when I visited. I recall its heaving pavement dotted with fat, sweaty stevedore-tourists in singlets and an aluminum public toilet with paper so harsh I cut myself badly and had to spend the rest of the day unable to explain to anyone why I was limping.

Getting off track here. After that, I grew ashamed. Bathrooms, with their fiddly bits, are one thing. But ceilings, walls, baseboards? I began painting. Not only could I not stop in mid-paint (somewhere there's a baseboard too far), but I couldn't stop thinking up things that needed painting. Furnace room floors, sheds, roofs, exterior trim, bedroom ceilings. Finally, S. told me to stop, said I was manic. I was bitterly resentful. I may be manic, but I'm handy,

I said. He objected to my silent, determined style of working, eschewing polite conversation. So I started painting when he left the house, desperately trying to finish in the hour he was grocery shopping but gaily aware that only one splash of paint would do. He'd have to let me finish the job after all. You can't have a garden shed with a big gaudy spot on it, like an archery target.

This was all a great improvement on my vacuuming fetish, as I hate lugging heavy canister vacuums and there is little satisfaction to be gained from a sucked and beaten carpet. And I love cleaning, but when my eyesight began failing at age forty, I realized that I was unlikely to spot a grime buildup where the taps meet their metal base, much less a long black hair in the bathtub in a house full of women with long black hair. This took some of the fun out of it. Oh, the painting obsession was a fleshy, satisfying thing. The colour spread like a lake in a rainstorm.

Preparing for trips not yet planned. This is truly absorbing. Tiny preparations are the biggest obstacle to going anywhere. You'd rather stay home, truth be told, than go downtown to duplicate your Hoon remover. The trick is to have all toiletries packed and ready to go, that is, travel-sized unguents and replacement makeup pots, medicines and tools. The idea is that aside from packing clothes, you're ready to go to Lisbon at the drop of a hat. The only drawback is that it is sheerest fantasy. You're not even able to go to the bank machine without forgetting your house keys and which shoes keep your pants out of puddles.

In extremis, I will sometimes go into stores and start straightening their goods on the shelves. A little rearranging of cereal boxes in the local supermarket was enough to stabilize me on one stressful morning of a beach vacation with the children. But the chaos that was one department store's Tower of Women's Jockey Underwear was so severe that I tidied and tidied until I was calm, though the thing still looked like a demolition site. Oddly, no salesclerk ever questioned me. Better her than me, they probably thought.

111. Embarrassing things

I greet a woman I recognize at a party with warmth, two seconds before realizing that she is a total stranger. Decide to keep up pretence. She, socially unsmooth, keeps insisting that we have never met and asks me questions—Who are you? What do you do for a living?—that compel me not just to identify myself but to justify my existence. I guess my M.A. was a waste of time, I find myself agreeing.

When I'm woken out of a deep sleep, I immediately say "Mummy!" When woken out of a very deep sleep, I call out "MummyMummyMummy." It's hellishly embarrassing on airplanes. One day I was asleep on the couch, woke up and said "Mummy!" "Yes, dear," said my mother who was sitting opposite me. I briefly considered explaining but it seemed too daft.

For years I have not had dreams, only terrible and endlessly inventive versions of the same nightmare. I am somewhere awful and cannot escape. Generally it's a workplace or a factory where I run from one torture to the next. Or I'll spend hours unable to find a cab while dogs eat my legs. It's that worst combination: horrid yet boring. Whoever's current in my life will sometimes show up. The De Quincey/Poe images come, endless traps surrounded by horrors, Vietnamese children with three eyes, suffering, bleeding damage and no possibility of escape. Something must be done. I vainly try to warn my doctor about how awful it is out there. She soothes me, saying Ssssshh. Her voice is very soft. I suppose she is my mother. The odd thing is that she is very, very good at it. In real life, she tells me I should exercise and get out of the house more.

112. I am entranced

I am entranced by British murder mysteries. In an episode of a series titled *Murder in Mind,* a blandly handsome pediatric surgeon with three perfect children and a lovely wife wakes up every night soaked in sweat and paralyzed by terror. He dreams of a little boy running through an autumn wood on a sunny day. The boy, seven, is terrified. As the dream advances each night, he realizes that he is not the boy being chased, but the nine-year-old doing the chasing. An older boy, eleven, is chasing along with him. The little boy trips and looks up, begging for mercy. A branch comes down. There is blood.

This is not a dream, the pediatrician knows in his bones. It really happened, a game of tag that turned hot and violent. He discovers that a boy disappeared in the neighbourhood thirty years ago and was never found. In his mother's photo albums, he finds the eleven-year-old boy who runs with him in the dream. His mother, confronted, says the older boy killed the child. He tracks down the older boy, now a grubby, suspicious odd-jobber, who says he didn't beat the child's brains in. It was you, he says. But I knew your mother would blame me and she said the police would too. So I shut up. It has haunted me for thirty years, he says. It has ruined my life.

The pediatrician goes to a police station and confesses to murder. Your mother has already confessed, they tell him. The boy fell down the stairs by accident and she panicked. The body is buried in her garden. We've found it.

And that's it. Thirty years later, he cannot prove that he killed the other child. No one will believe the other man, who is working class, not an immaculate pediatrician. Instead, they believe the pediatrician's nice old mum. The doctor knows his mother is covering for him, but he can't prove it. Even though he still thinks he was the killer, he can do nothing. It's over. Done. Perhaps there will be peace, of a sort.

And the next night, he wakes up coated in sweat and rigid with terror. The dream is back. It will never leave his mind. It's his own little murder and it will return every night of his life. His tragedy is that he will never be punished.

It's a torture worthy of Dostoevsky. We all live with the knowledge of our own guilt and deceit, while the rest of the world happily treats us as normal, decent citizens. In their misunderstanding lies the turn of the vise. People like us are never believed. We get away with murder every day.

113. Things you can do without

Norwalk virus has you on your hands and knees after Christmas dinner, assessing whether the string of orange tissue you have shot from your throat is smoked salmon or part of a mandarin orange. Sadly, you will have little else to contemplate for another seven hours. Towards the end, you conclude that it may well have been part of your stomach lining. How fortunate that one's stomach is anchored, so to speak, at its nether end. Because one's body is clearly doing its best to propel it in the opposite direction.

There are churches everywhere in the city, just as there are blue jays and robins, if you could be bothered to notice them. But they're stale, tired-looking buildings that know they're on a list the wreckers haven't got to yet, good for nothing but hatchings, matchings and dispatchings.

Reading your teenage diaries. Opening one at random, I read, "He was apologetic. Control. Self-possession. Arrogance. God help me. Please. Don't let him hurt me." What on earth was I on about? I couldn't have been more than fifteen. Such were the joys.

114. Things that make one wary

At the moment we are obsessed with hair. Let me correct that. Someone is obsessed. I now watch only taped TV shows so that I can skip the ads. But when I can't, I am tormented by the number of commercials for shampoos and conditioners and goops that make women's hair swirl, sweep, cascade, fly, flow, ripple, blow, gleam ... Hair everywhere, a thousand brands of unguents to choose from. It's only hair, I think, which I did not think when I was a teenage girl. But I notice very little spectacular hair in the city where I live. Shiny manes so thick and perfect that they weigh down a woman's head? Nope. Perhaps they just left whatever room I happened to be in. Perhaps they are at home, grooming and retooling for the evening ahead.

Before seeing Barry Humphries's/Dame Edna Everage's stage show in New York, I order chicken fingers in an awful chrome-walled bar on Broadway. What arrives is tubelike, but it doesn't appear to be chicken. It could be anything—shrimp, denatured pork product, breaded tarmac. Worse, it could be these things with more conviction than it could be chicken. I am so intrigued by my mystery meat that I can't be upset by having to pay for it.

With my full consent, a stepdaughter is expelled from summer camp for various sins, one of them being hiding a tub of peanut butter in her tent. The counsellors warned that peanut butter would attract bears of which there are many in the nearby woods. That same year, a man I once knew well buttered his toast with a knife that had a taste, a hint, of peanut butter. He stopped breathing and died. Could anything be more mundane than Skippy Smooth and Skippy Nutty and yet so lethal?

115. Domestic things that create order

Tightening the sagging hessian fence that guards the front hedge from the salt spray of the road.

Cleaning the surface of the computer which builds up a black tan for no reason I can see. Its plastic attracts black dirt like a magnet. But why? I'm told it is static. I nod knowingly. What is static?

Using Q-Tips to clean tight small corners. You're forty and you've never done this before. Has your life been a story of unnoticed tiny compacted filth?

116. When I need private comfort

When I need private comfort, I marvel at the work that went into sustaining and coddling my stepdaughters' bodies when they were little. I knew every inch of them, every crevice, every curve from head to toe. I washed, rinsed and dried their hair, had it cut, cleaned their faces and ears, taught them how to blow their noses (why do toddlers so resent this?) and put ointment on their sores. Their teeth were taken to dentists, feet to orthotic specialists, skin to dermatologists. Torso time: I bought all their clothes, including the white knickers and vests that little girls wear, and later, stacks of grown-up underwears, as they called them. I bought them a thousand socks, dozens of track shoes and purple Doc Martens in Covent Garden. When one child broke her leg, I signed her cast and photographed her in the purple lightweight cast that delighted her. I pierced their ears and deplored their tattoos, taught them how to shave their legs, moisturize skin, pluck eyebrows, treat blemishes and wear makeup.

It was pleasurable, but at some level dreadful. Corporeally, I owned them. Yet they still speak to me, love me even. I would deeply resent anyone who had this level of control over my body. There's something chain-gang-ish about it, as though their bodies were my private property. It offends me and I still can't understand why they haven't fled the woman who controlled their skin and bones like some kind of puppetmaster. I would.

117. Jade Goody

I was desperately upset by a reality show in Britain called *Big Brother* in which various foolish and vulnerable people were filmed twenty-four hours a day in a house in which they were locked. Weekly, one would be voted out. One young inmate was Jade Goody. She was overweight and had exaggerated features, including full lips and a broad upturned nose. She wasn't very bright and her desire to be liked was palpable, which made her painfully vulnerable to bullying by the other contestants. Reality shows attract a lower class of human. Crowds were showing up at the house with signs saying "Kill the pig."

As it turns out, Jade was born in poverty. Her father, who was black and who bequeathed the features that so offended the crowd, had abandoned the family early. She dressed in sexy clothes, wanting to appeal to men, but it seemed to enrage them. Her femaleness, her "differentness," brought out a blood hunger in viewers.

I read about these events and was struck dumb with grief and pity. I wanted to write about Jade and what impulse makes humans want to kick Jades to death. I talked to another woman about this. She herself looked a little like Jade, dark, slightly overweight and with the turned-up nose that exposes the interior of the nostrils, and she was frequently mocked for her stupidity. I assumed she would be kind to the young woman, but she responded coldly, saying of Jade, "She is painfully disgusting to watch—stupid, ugly and weak."

This is the essence of bullying. If Jade were lying in the street, you'd kick her breasts and buttocks because your own tits and ass have been mocked. You'd boot her in the head because you have been called stupid. And you'd know that secretly you are weak, so you'd kick her extra hard for that. The stupid, ugly and weak are the worst offenders when it comes to mugging the stupid, ugly and weak.

The whole incident seemed unremarkable on the surface, but in the dark it unspooled like a Sergio Leone western about women.

118. Things that make one's heart beat faster

Blowing a grand.

Being attacked by a malicious, ill-read, inept writer. When you realize that you can't possibly respond, this person being such a clot that it's beneath you to take notice, your heartbeat returns to normal. Why can't you be attacked by someone you respect?

Getting a black and white enamelled Kenneth Jay Lane bracelet from S., presented to you at the restaurant table with champagne. You're breathing hard with delight and thinking, What went right in the store? Is there a chance he could be trained for next year? And then you dismiss these cartilaginous thoughts and go all soft again for this man who so dislikes shopping, who went so thoroughly against his own grain to give you pleasure.

119. Things that arouse a fond memory of the past

One-night stands that stayed that way. The trick is not to know his surname.

120. Things that give a pathetic impression

It is a truth that anyone who ever had a brush with Hitler and his gang will write their memoirs and invariably say, If only I had shot him, how different our lives would have been, sigh. Alec Guinness does it about Goebbels and Goering passing in a car in 1939; the entire Mitford family goggled at Hitler in a restaurant (and some of them had a gun on them!); an actor thinks an ancestor may have given Hitler a much-needed overcoat once. Everyone appears to have run into him somewhere but, sadly, left their machete in their other briefcase. What nonsense. You cannot even approach correctly predicting the consequences of such an act. Maybe worse things would have happened, a Hitler clone with the wit to oppose wars fought on two fronts. The only certain thing is that you would have personally suffered a prolonged death that would never be written about in the history books despite your shot at stardom. You saw an ugly star and you blew it.

How does this sound? S. remembers the Letts family that ran an electrical shop in Northam in North Devon. The serial killer Rosemary West was one of their daughters. I used to see their van, he says. Maybe her dad did your electrical work, I say. No, my dad was a real handyman, did everything himself. That's a shame, I say. Some quick work with a few wires, the van explodes and West wouldn't have been born and Martin Amis, one of whose relatives was killed by West, would have written one fewer stupid book. What a riveting anecdote this is. See?

121. Sea change at full fathom five

Those who say digitalization has altered our lives forever are aiming slam bang at the most obvious changes. The computer on which I write this is still basically a typewriter with a wonderful facility for moving paragraphs around. I write plenty of emails, but I used to write pounds of letters.

No, what has changed the most is the fact that when I was in grade school in a small town in northwestern Ontario, we were taken to see a travelling show of transvestite dwarves. I still remember the man's almost full-sized head, looking as though his forehead had been ironed so that his head sloped from a point at the back. He wore a pale blue chiffon dress with ruffles at the collar and down-the-front buttons, which in the 1960s was what women wore. What I cannot forget was his big male mouth, coated in bright red lipstick, as he sang and danced. As a result, I have an aversion to clowns, to the public humiliation of little people, to big, wet lips; name an aversion and it likely springs from this memory. But the real significance of this man who was child-sized being forced to dance for children is that it signals the biggest change of my lifetime. In 2004, this would not be considered a suitable class trip.

122. Things go awry

Things go awry when you phone computer helplines and you vow never to do it again, until the memory of the last debacle fades and you do it again. I call the Dell helpline at 6:15 P.M., secure in the knowledge that dinner isn't until seven which is plenty of time for Dell to explain why the little x in the upper-right-hand corner of the screen is in hiding, beyond the reach of the cursor unless I want to make a wild guess which I don't really.

So I call Dell and after listening to a menu that is entirely incomprehensible to me—am I a Dagatron or a Pedopod—I end up talking to the wrong person who forwards my call to another wrong person.

She and I do a thousand things together, none of which I understand and none of which work. But she is insistent on one thing: she must have my service tag number. It is on the bottom of the laptop which is plugged into a dozen cords and ports at the back and thus cannot be pulled out of its wooden slot on my desk without the system presumably disintegrating. I rely on a keyboard and a monitor. I never touch the laptop, which cannot be lifted more than two inches anyway inside its little pine home, so the service tag with its twenty digits that are too small for me to read anyway might as well be on the surface of the moon.

But the young woman has an accent. Where are you, I ask. She's in India. Yes, Dell is one of the most profitable American computer makers, partly because it has exported its call centres to India. I'm in Canada, I say. I feel very guilty. In India, women are treated as house slaves and I know she needs my service tag number. Maybe she'll lose her job. Maybe her husband's family will turn against her, as in a Ruth Prawer Jhabvala novel, or heaven forbid, a Rohinton Mistry, and make her life a hot waterless hell. She may lose her legs to gangrene and slide around on a trolley begging for rice for the next thirty years. Millions clamour for her job. She needs my service tag number.

So. I put on my reading glasses, raise the front edge of the laptop as high as I can and with the aid of a magnifying glass try to decipher the numbers. They are upside down. So I find a small mirror with a handle, turn it to its magnifying side and by means of another mirror, try to reflect the numbers right side up while enlarging them.

Then S. calls out that dinner is ready: organic baby beef liver cooked to a Nigel Slater recipe that requires time, timing and skill. Having just read the Dinner of Revenge scene in Jonathan Franzen's *The Corrections,* and as well recalling my own meatloaf memories from childhood, I know that liver brooks no delay. S. is furious.

I have four glass gadgets plus a laptop in my two hands with my head twisted upside down and the Indian lady on speaker phone telling me that the number does not register anywhere on her list.

My dinner's ready, I say plaintively. My husband is calling me. I figure she'll sympathize coming from a culture where men are bullies. But no, she needs that service tag. I beg. Please let me have my dinner. Here's my number. Can you call me in half an hour and we'll try again? Please? Eventually, wracked by guilt I hang up, give up and run down to dinner where I rhapsodize over a liver platter that has been kept warming in the oven for fifteen minutes. I'm so sorry, mmmmmm! this is so good. I'm sorry, I was talking to India, my, this is delicious (which, amazingly, it is).

India never does call back, the little x still disappears on a whim and I will never call any helpline again on a subject on which I have no expertise. I will leave it to S.

But I leave you with this: Why are they called helplines?

123. One writer's greatest fear

Bill Bryson, the travel writer, confesses as he clumps around Britain in muddy boots that his greatest fear is that, when he takes a walk in the countryside, he has no witnesses to speak up for him should he be charged with a murder. He's always looking around for his alibi. I saw that tree, he'll remind himself. Then he'll remember that the tree didn't see him. What he needs is a conversation with humans—picnickers, say. The fact that he hasn't committed a murder is somehow not relevant. After all, the naked corpses of young women are always being found here and there. I was in the woods, he'll tell the police officers in vain. No one saw me.

I don't worry about this, perhaps because I am a woman and more likely to be one of the corpses. No, my fate is to be an eyewitness. I'll see something a little abnormal, take a wild chance and follow a white van (Theodore Bundy used a white van for his last murder, you see) to a grubby bungalow on the outskirts of the city. I will alert the police to strange goings-on. At first, I will be considered mad. But when the body of a kidnapped girl is found in the house, I will be the one with information that might be vital. I will be stalwart in the witness box.

I note that the man fears he cannot prove the facts of his existence. I, on the other hand, fear that I will not be able to prove my good intentions, which will appear useless, even absurd. Do you always prowl after people's vehicles for no goddamn reason, I'll be asked.

124. Worrying things

Each year the house's water pressure becomes slightly less. The shower is more of a spray than a blast. In the spring, the sprinkler's reach grows ever shorter, which means I have to run outside five times a day and move it about the lawn to get all the parched bits. Soon, it won't be a sprinkler. It'll spurt, then dribble, then dry up. No metaphors here. This isn't global warming, just my pipes.

125. Depressing things

There's an organization called Looking Good, Feeling Better. It coaches women with cancer on how to wear makeup and wigs, get manicures and pedicures and develop a positive attitude. "Lipstick can brighten your look and lift your spirits." This enrages me. Of all the times in my life when I would feel entitled to look as bad as I felt, cancer would be that time. I suppose childbirth is the other. It's hard enough to keep yourself in good nick when you're healthy. But the nagging follows you to the grave. I mean, *piss off.*

All that is beige is hateful to me. What a sad sack era of interior decoration. A design consultant suggests I paint my house trim in taupe. Instead, I paint it in a rich forest green. Later I walk by her little shop of housey things. The store and everything in it is taupe. My neighbour paints over her pretty blue trim in a peculiar beige. I suddenly realize that it is the colour of Band-Aids, in other words flesh-coloured but not a flesh possessed by any human. The rest of the wood she paints woodlice brown. I hate brown. It's just beige in bulk.

I frequently give books as gifts to people I think might appreciate them. For books are healing drugs and should be handed out like pastilles. But I have rarely received one in return. It wouldn't occur to most people, even though it is the most graceful gesture that it is possible to make.

I am shy about my amateur interests, which are figurative painting, and architecture, and writers most people would consider obscure. At a fundraising dinner, I find myself talking to a mutual fund manager about Émile Zola for some reason and am astonished to discover that he knows a great deal about him. It's unfair to assume that a man with a keen and instinctive knowledge of the stock market wouldn't be interested in French novelists, but I'm afraid I do think this.

As we babble about *Germinal* and *Thérèse Raquin* and all things Zola, it becomes apparent that he knows a great deal more than I do. Secretly I know that my ambition to read all the Rougon-Macquart novels in French will never be fulfilled, but it is still so pleasant to have this conversation. Days later, he couriers to me a video copy of *Germinal* starring Gérard Depardieu. I am delighted. And yet I still berate myself. I am so used to people's antipathy towards intellect and so unaccustomed to talking openly to strangers about the artists I love that it would be easier for me to strip naked in public than to say any of these words out loud: *Pamela; Shamela;* Hotspur; Rego; Thiebaud; Wieland; "Commoditie, Firmeness, and Delight." They are code words to my secret passions and telling them to a stranger is like talking dirty or finding someone with whom you can converse in Esperanto. You whisper together.

I cannot get over the generosity of this man. I squirm with embarrassment. I bet I pronounced Rougon-Macquart wrong. I bet it's a hard "g," not a soft one, I think to myself at 2 A.M. He probably thinks I'm a Zola airhead.

Am I ever going to give myself a break?

126. Admirable things

On the news, I watch the current wave of forest fires spread across the continent. It must be embarrassing, along with great, when your town burns down after weeks of wild forest fires, and your house is one of the few left standing. It's looking bloody good. Even the shrubs are untouched. People invited the burned-out into their immaculate homes. Would I have done this? Or would I have said "Here's some family pictures for you. I know you lost all yours. I never liked my family anyway." One hopes one is never tested.

My girlfriend's passionate love for her children, despite three childbirths that all went wrong for some reason, usually medical incompetence and the indifference of nurses. Yet she strokes the hair on her daughter's head, the head that got stuck coming out and wouldn't budge. And she remembers the IV that hit the wrong spot on her hand so they went for a second stab, blowing the hand up like a balloon and causing her husband to collapse. She says, by the way, that it's a lie that you forget the pain.

127. Family themes

Every family has one, even if it isn't aware of it. Ours was "There's more to life than pleasure," which Glaswegian-ly still rings in my brain. A friend's family were heavy drinkers, their theme "None of us gets out of here alive." Isadora Wing, Erica Jong's heroine in *Fear of Flying,* says hers was "The world is a predatory place. Eat faster!" Calvin Trillin, humorist and gourmet, invented the notion of the "theme," which is not the same as a motto. He says his family theme as Jews growing up in Kansas City was "We have worked hard so that you can have the opportunity to be a real American." For his own kids, whom they raised in New York City, it was "Despite appearances to the contrary, you are being raised in Kansas City."

I will helpfully give you space. Think hard.

Your family theme:

---

128. Things that are distant though near

You are in your house and it is your house, safe as houses. But if you are out at 3 A.M. and walking silently along your street in the June warmth, it is as if you are a teenager again and you see all the houses as you once saw the houses of your parents and your friends' parents, powerful houses, solid and yet mysterious. This is where I live, you'd think. But I don't recognize it. I now know that there is no such thing in this world as glamour. But at sixteen, everything shimmers with it. Established grown-ups live here, and I am fresh and young and waiting for the world to happen to me. At 3 A.M., with insomnia, I used to be calmed by the sight of my stepchildren sleeping. I am obsessed with interiors now, not those once-glamorous exteriors.

129. Things that fall from the sky

Rain

Snow

Frozen green urine from airplanes

Twin Towers

Prosthetic legs in Afghanistan in the film *Kandahar*

Junk food parcels and bombs in nations the U.S. wants to destroy while becoming popular. Trick or treat! The Americans behave like an abusive husband who is contrite in the morning and pours out cereal for his bruised wife.

Cheques for writing. Writing is not work. It is in its own class of the economy, a gift and not a commodity, as the theorist Lewis Hyde says. I never relate the money to the words that pulled in the cheque and often feel I am being paid as compensation for the rudeness of the newspaper copy editor who was landed with the piece and out of resentment gave me the Full Brazilian.

130. Things that should be equal but are not

We are told that it is human nature to like symmetrical faces. But my breasts aren't quite the same size. Most women's aren't. The problem with breasts is that there is no way to conceal them. They're there, secondary sexual characteristics, sticking out, one big and blowsy, one less so. They have nowhere to hide.

The extraordinary tidiness of Vita Sackville-West's garden at Sissinghurst. Virginia and Leonard Woolf's garden is, in contrast, a mess. But it's more personal. Nothing better illustrates the difference between VW's writing and Vita's "pen of brass."

131. Unwise things

To forestall an argument in a French restaurant, I suggest S. and I play Desert Island Discs. It turns out that mine are all about love—Carly Simon's *Forever My Love,* Eric Carmen's *Sunrise,* Ronstadt's *Long Long Time* and Roxy Music's *Running Wild*—and his are all about nostalgia and loss—Van Morrison's *These Are the Days,* Neil Young's *Helpless,* the Stones' *The Last Time,* Carole King's *Ain't That the Way* and The Righteous Brothers' *You've Lost That Loving Feeling.* What's puzzling is that we have traded places. S. is the least nostalgic person I know. His motto is "No rearview mirror." But he is romantic, at least about this marriage. And I am cynical about romantic love, but paralyzed by my yearning for the past. Something's out of whack. We're both on the wrong soundtrack. Or are we lying to ourselves?

Do not impatiently tug the lawnmower cord out of its socket with jerking motions from twenty metres away because you can't be arsed to go to the source. The sight of a three-prong plug shooting directly towards your eyeball at great speed is not one you wish to revisit. Luckily, it strikes your hard head, not one of your two soft, pretty, essential vision balls protected only by a browbone and a lid.

132. Things that arouse suspicion

Like everyone else, I get thousands of emails asking if I want my male organ enlarged. But I was taken aback to get an email asking if I wanted to see a woman grow large breasts.

For I have already seen a woman grow large breasts. It wasn't even a coincidence. It happened to me personally. How can something so mundane become a commodity for the other sex?

They aerated my lawn today with this huge electrified roller ball with protruding metal spikes—simply Inquisitional, as the late great Robert Palmer might say. Then they reseeded the whole mess and a lawn guy named Jim left me a lengthy handwritten note warning me to keep my lawn "moist for a period of twenty-eight days." Maybe I'm paranoid after all those emails but do you think the guy really means my *lawn?* Even if he does, who *moistens* their lawn? In my world, they water them. And why does it have to be moist for a *period* of time that matches the exact length of my menstrual cycle? Why not just write "Water your lawn daily for a month"? The form says my seeds will dry out. I wish they would. Then I wouldn't have to take these damn pills twenty-one days a month as I have for the past twenty-four years. Also, I don't think I can stay constantly sexually aroused for four weeks.

As I say, maybe I'm being paranoid here.

Anyway, lawn sprinkling is my husband's responsibility. Husbands (and mine is the one who came up with this theory) are by definition responsible for three things: bugs, bags and bogs. Their job is to kill the bugs, carry heavy bags and fix a running toilet. Add to that turning the lawn into a swamp or *bog*.

133. I am writing upstairs

I am writing upstairs while S. gardens and his daughter watches TV in the basement. Noises, thuds. V. calls. Daddy needs help. I run outside. S. is standing with his arm and hand held stiff and vertical. Blood covers his arm, the gate, the door, as in the Manson murders. Later, I am unable to remove the stains that have soaked into the wood.

I've cut off my fingertip, he says. His little finger stops suddenly. It is squared off. I don't see a fingernail. Apparently he was trimming the burning bush at the foot of the pergola and thinking about problems with his other teenage daughter. He cut down hard with his secateurs (manual, not electric) and severed his own finger.

We search the flowerbed for the missing tip without success. "Oh my god, there it is," V. says. (I am still grateful to her for finding it, as I suspect I wouldn't have, and it would have been left there to rot.) And there it is, a small pink thing. She can't bear to pick it up, so I do. We wrap his finger in gauze, place the tip on ice and drive to the hospital.

In the confusion we are sent, wrongly, to another hospital. The only transport is a hearse and the driver offers to take us, saying, via a euphemism I have blocked out, that he has space for us.

We spend six hours at the hospital emergency room, which is chaotic and filthy. I repeatedly beg for ice for the fingertip. Eventually, a good-humoured, inept junior doctor, the kind of person who'd have difficulty purchasing a movie ticket from one of those machines (it's new but you should have learned by now), fails to sew on S.'s fingertip, which ferments for six weeks and withers wetly away.

It must be dressed morning and night with an elaborate arrangement of gauze soaked in distilled water followed by gauze soaked in ointment and then bandages cut in the shape of the holy cross. The only bright spot is that if S. and I argue, the argument ceases upon the point of dressing and bandaging. Hostilities are suspended for the duration of the procedure. It is difficult for me to hold a grudge against a man with a finger like that. And he can hardly be cross with a woman who attends to his finger with a discipline and devotion that would win praise from Florence Nightingale. Okay, Nurse Cherry Ames.

Now he has a stump. Occasionally I refer to the innocence of the pink thing lying in the muck of the flowerbed, just to make everyone writhe.

134. Christmas is the worst time to die

Christmas is the worst time to die because unless you were spectacularly awful while alive, your relatives will be forced to start reliving the agony of your death as soon as the first red bow goes up on a plastic wreath, which is right after Halloween. They will associate carols, gift shopping, tree management and once-yearly comestibles with hearing the news, touching the cold, pale face and burying the corpse (not until spring!). The season becomes not only demanding, but sinister. Ho-ho-ho becomes a cackle of glee at black blood. Red is the colour of blood, you suddenly realize.

And people frequently die at Christmas, shovelling snow, overeating, overdrinking, oversmoking or pasted into the road by a drunken driver. I think of it as a time when men die.

It was just before midnight on Victoria Day in the spring when my mother called me to tell me my father had died. This wouldn't have been bad timing, had the Victoria Day fireworks not started going off on the lakeshore as soon as she said the words. I love fireworks but I no longer go to see them.

Worse, Victoria Day is a floating holiday, so whenever I hear the fireworks they remind me of distant horror that isn't justified because he didn't die on that precise day anyway.

135. Specimen Day

I always record Specimen Days in my diary. They are days picked at random, like a drug test, and they give a flavour of how we were living at that time. Also, they tend to be packed with worthwhile activity and thus give a satisfactorily misleading view of my life, which is laziness incarnate.

"House & garden, house & garden. This morning, I upped and mowed the lawn, trimmed the edges by hand and watered. Huge fast thundery rainstorm with a river running down the hill road. Made a curry and bread, ordered garden tools, paid bills, read a foot-high stack of Brit papers and some of Virginia Woolf's chewing on old bones. I am reading Liz Tilberis's *No Time to Die* (but she did, leaving behind troubling warnings about fertility drugs and how the ovary can only be asked to fire eggs so many times without its rebelling), Simon Schama's *Landscape & Memory* and *Just Checking,* an extraordinary memoir by Emily Colas about obsessive-compulsive disorder. She writes about all the things she imagines could go wrong, none of which would have occurred to the rest of us who are wrapped in bad things that are highly plausible, indeed imminent. In Miranda France's prescient *Bad Times in Buenos Aires,* everyone in the city takes tranquillizers and sees psychoanalysts they can't afford. They were right to worry, for the economy collapsed in 1999. A current magazine feature profiles the residents who survived psychologically. One man had set up a rental service for armoured cars. People travel 30 km to sell their hair to wig factories. All the survivors had hard faces. They had learned to barter rather than buy."

136. Ridiculous things

In my third year, I was taught an English Literature course by the great Northrop Frye. His lectures flowed. A man without ego, he was always courteous to students. On the one day when he was being photographed for a magazine cover, he was patient. Then he concealed his impatience. Then he made a gesture that summed up the irritation he felt at being photographed for a magazine cover when he was busy teaching students about the Biblical pattern in the background of our literature. He gave me a B– on my essay on T.S. Eliot which was generous in the extreme. For such is my allergic dislike of religion that I was unable to take in a single thing he said about the Biblical pattern in the background of our literature. He had a cargo plane of knowledge about it that completely eluded me.

A demonstrator against the American invasion of Iraq is photographed in London holding up a sign "Down with this sort of thing." The photo is flashed around the world to signify everything—English wit, pacifism—but what it actually signifies. It is a line from the TV comedy *Father Ted,* TV critic John Doyle reminds me. Some allegedly blasphemous anti-Catholic piece of filth was being shown at the cinema on Craggy Island and Ted, told he should do something, showed up with the idiot Father Dougal carrying a sign saying "Down with this sort of thing."

Will provincial department stores ever die out? Or do they quietly tick-tock away forever? I remember Bucovetsky's in Kapuskasing with its one shelf of felt hats, and Chopes in Bideford in North Devon with half a dozen raggle-taggle rooms on slightly different levels so you kept tripping. It sold things you sort of maybe needed like kettles and baby socks and huge cheap suitcases for men in the motor trade who have been thrown out by their embittered wives and are moving into a room above the pub. At the counter, they had a rack of rubber swimming caps with rubber flanges like the fringes of sea anemones and big rubber daisies, the most splendid collection of such things I have ever seen. To this day, I curse not having bought one as I worry that no one will ever believe they existed unless I can hold one out and show how the thing trembles and wiggles in my hand like a squid being electrocuted. S. disliked the family that owned Chopes. They were snobbish, he said, and clearly felt they were Bideford's mercantile upper crust.

A woman in a British country-house hotel comes down to dinner in a dress cut so that one breast is revealed, deliberately, to the entire room. Her nipple is reddish and medium-sized as is her breast. The stepchildren are choking with laughter.

We are eating in a hotel dining room. "Know what my favourite word is? Feces!" my little stepdaughter announces gaily. She said later that my face changed.

"That's disgusting!" I roar. I have never felt so much like a big old mum out of a Beryl Cook painting.

"Why? What does it mean?" She's starting to look panicky.

"Poo!"

The kids explode with horror and laughter.

137. Things to which there is no response

I am having lunch with two older women who have known each other for decades. Our Thai lunch arrives at the table. My friend eats a little and excuses herself for a moment. "That can't have gone through you that fast," her companion bellows. My friend is speechless. I suppose the answer is never to tell anyone when you have bowel problems as everything you do will then be interpreted in that light.

In a speech, Seymour M. Hersh points out an oddity: We demand complete integrity in our personal lives but none in our political leaders. This is true. We cannot explain it. We are struck dumb. Bush lying about his reasons for invading Iraq is like lying to your husband that you have landed a high-paying job in Tennessee or

Guatemala so you have to move there. And when you get there it's 40°C in the shade and there are patches of blood all over the driveway of your new house and the kids have monkeypox and you tell him there's no job but, gee, you expect to find one any year now. He'll divorce you for that. But Americans shrug about a little war based on lies, as if Georgie, as his mother calls him, is going through "a phase" so be patient.

A woman friend tells me she has signed a contract to write a novel, the most difficult form of writing at which to succeed. A great, or even a good novel, cannot put one foot wrong. She has never written a word of fiction before. Now we are both authoresses, she trills. I am a diarist at best, I think. She, on the other hand, is facing two years of self-sodomy with a pink fist. *Authoress.*

"Start spreadin' the news … I'm leavin' today … New York, New York." A band plays brassy American show tunes in the Piazza San Marco in Venice.

138. Things that are inescapable

If you visit a museum in a foreign city and see a work of art that entrances you, you must realize that if they don't have that postcard in the gift shop, it will be lost from your life forever. There isn't a thing you can do. Certain museums have art to burn and are casual about it. I am thinking of a Clodion bas relief in the Louvre of babies playing in a forest and a Museo Correr painting of Venetian tumblers on a medieval version of a trampoline. I will likely not see you babies, you bouncers, again.

139. Disturbing things

You are a middle-aged woman entering your hotel room after a flight. You unpack, placing your belongings, of which there are far too many, around the room just so. It's a nice room, better than you deserve, really. You are being paid generously to speak in public, something that seems slightly absurd, but you have agreed to it because you like to keep moving. It helps you avoid depression.

You go downstairs and sit alone in the dining room, eating soup and reading the book you chose as company, Margaret Drabble's *The Realms of Gold*. It begins with a middle-aged woman entering her hotel room after a flight and unpacking. The room's too good for the likes of her, she thinks. She is making a speech in this city. Why? To keep moving, to avoid depression. The book mirrors you exactly, even down to the soup and the fact that you are worried about a tooth. It could be worse, you think. At least it's a civilized Drabble. It could have been an Ian McEwan novel and you'll get chopped up by a pair of sexual deviants for the crime of being polite to them.

San Diego's climate is heavenly. Not too hot, not too cold, with a breeze off the ocean that's just right. Sunny, but not enough that sunglasses are called for. You needn't fret over bringing a sweater. Whatever you wear will be just right for this day which is pleasant as a matter of weather policy. As the days pass, you visit an attractive mall with every store that is always found in every mall in the U.S. There's a Williams-Sonoma, a Pottery Barn, a Bridgestone. The Museum of Natural History is on its last legs. You visit a "village" where Mexican "crafts" are sold. They are like the gifts that children make in school, but made by white geriatrics. There isn't anything genuinely Spanish in sight, but there are a lot of Made in Hong Kong serapes and highly coloured mud ashtrays shaped like birds. What there isn't is a bookstore. San Diego manages without them. San Diego is an American daydream on the outside, a nightmare once you think about it. Life there is death in slow motion.

I have bought a new bed for my tiny niece, who has been out of her crib for only a few months. I am stripping the old bed in preparation for assembling the new one. She catches me at it. Her bed is her world. Stop! Stop! she cries in anguish. Huge waves of anger and outrage gush from this tiny person who looks about eighteen inches tall. I stop instantly and apologize profusely. I am shattered. She takes her mother's hand and leaves the room, her chest heaving. In her absence, I construct the new bed (world), which is ample and pretty. The old bed (world) is gone without a trace. When she returns, she accepts this without a murmur.

140. People you would feel obliged to attack in restaurants

Henry Kissinger in New York. This happens apparently. War criminal, angry diners shout as they are hustled out the door. Surely the wrong person is being ejected.

General Augusto Pinochet lunching at Fortnum & Mason in Piccadilly. I used to stop in there after buying great stacks of books at Hatchards. It was convenient but mainly I enjoyed watching the chaos of the restaurant, which was almost choreographed. You never got what you ordered. You could wait an hour for your scones, your tea, your bill. You could walk out without paying every single day and no one would notice. Then I read about Pinochet lunching there in the year before he was arrested for war crimes. A boiling pot of hot tea over his head would be quite the thing, but they would have lost your tea order anyway.

He won't leave Chile now lest he be arrested again. Neither will Kissinger leave the U.S. It isn't me they fear. But they should. I do seethe at the sight of things. Now, of course, I never go back to Fortnum. I see bloodstains on the minty green walls. I've read the testimony of those Pinochet ordered tortured in Chile, how a torture victim smells and comes to hate his smell, and thereby himself, which is the torturers' intention. Fortnum smells bad now.

141. Things I cannot quite believe

The American humorist David Sedaris writes that his younger brother Paul, a Cro-Magnon from South Carolina, has an elderly pug dog and a Great Dane. As David and Paul walked on the beach after Paul's wedding, David watched the little dog emit a mound of peanut-sized turds. Rather than clean it up himself, Paul whistled for his Great Dane who ran over and enthusiastically ate the shit. Not only had he trained the dog to do this, Paul boasted, but sometimes "he'll stick his nose to her ass and just eat that shit on tap."

Now David, I love you. You may be the funniest man in the United States. I bought copies of your book *Naked* for all my friends. But please tell me you made that story up. Even if you didn't make it up, please tell me you made that story up.

A work friend asks me to dinner at her house. Attending will be a man she has dined with once. He would not sleep with her. But he has agreed to come to her home as long as I will be there too. This man is a gun owner and quite strange.

I refuse as politely as I can. I am simply amazed that she would think I'd even consider showing up for an evening that has a Stephen King ending written all over it or that she wouldn't think S. would object. I hate the word "husband" but never has it seemed more comforting. As a result, she never speaks to me again.

I tell this story to a girlfriend. "Omigod, you're a fluffer," she shrieks. A fluffer is a woman whose function on the set of a porn movie is to keep the male actors erect so they can continue to prang the female actors who do not inspire erections.

A woman tells me, as we play with her happy little daughter, the story of her mother, L—. L—'s own mother died in childbirth and L—, the ostensible cause of it, was abandoned by her father. She was raised by her grandmother in the same small town as her father and two brothers. When her father saw her, he would cross the street. My friend's mother grew up unable to love, although apparently she can feign it. My friend, a warm happy person whom I like immensely, can spot L— faking grandmotherly and motherly behaviour. She won't visit sick relatives but will attend funerals. The dead demand nothing of her.

My editor shows me the cover photo from the magazine that went out on the weekend, a photo of a bike courier. "Do you notice anything about this picture?" he says grimly. I stare, I search. "Nope." He points. The courier's piece of prime is hanging outside his denim shorts, the entire young pink length of it. By the end of the day, we have received almost no phone calls of complaint. Out of some unconscious courtesy, such sights don't register with the public or with me. Over them the polite eye passes.

We look down from our balcony table at the parking valet at a Barcelona restaurant. He parks cars so that they block other cars and then extracts them by crashing them, one, two, three, into other cars. He does this repeatedly, damaging half a dozen vehicles. We watch the results as people come out to collect their cars—the fed-up father, the amused wife, the non-helpful teenagers, the smug valet, the debating passersby. It's like watching a Feydeau farce. Doors are slamming as they do on stage, but in this one, the comedy is hammered out by car doors.

An American tourist is sitting with his wife and the model-handsome young man who crews their yacht. The tourist looks like George C. Scott. He is meaty and tanned and badly marked by vitiligo. The young man sings for his supper, recounting his treatment of the rest of the crew. "I told Karen, I said I like women who are young, intelligent and good-looking and you are none of those three." The vitiligo man's wife is old and ugly in a brassy way. She sits silently. The couple is served first. The vitiligo man claps his hands loudly and directs a waiter to the young man's empty plate. The young Spanish waiter is hurt and angry, for one does not treat a Catalan in this manner. S. interprets the scene for me. He says the young man has been hired to sleep with the old wife. Every remark he makes is designed to bait her in front of her husband, who is preoccupied with humiliating the waiter. They are a hateful group. There is nothing more excruciating than rich surgeried Americans out in public following their script.

My girlfriend tells me her mother was a midwife in South Africa at a home for unwed mothers. In those days, they made a specialty of treating such girls badly, à la Magdalene Laundries in Ireland. Just as the woman went into labour, the midwife would say to her, "In like a banana, out like a pineapple."

142. Things that give a clean feeling

A genuine sun-kissed full-body tan, which I will never have again.

My tiny niece, refusing to eat her tomato soup in a restaurant. She smashes her lips closed and shakes her head with finality. I am struck by how much I love to see girls say NO. It is healthy. And tragically, it will not last.

Lester Maddox and Strom Thurmond die within a day of each other. Talk about unlooked-for happiness.

143. Things that give an unclean feeling

I visit Versailles. It has two thousand rooms, fifteen of which are open to the public, which shows what the French think of tourists. Approaching the ramparts, I see that the forecourt of the huge building is blocked by tour buses, at least fifty of them. Just getting in the palace requires patience and determination but once in, you're in with ten thousand geriatric American tourists. They are massively fat in their golfwear, white sneakers and fanny packs. I'm not claustrophobic and am as interested in Louis XIV as the next person, but inside the Hall of Mirrors, there's gridlock. Old fat people pile up. The normal human sixth sense about personal space has been lost because we can't move. It's very hot, like "festival seating" at a Stones concert, but the fans are ancient Brobdingnags and I am crushed by breasts, bellies and buttocks. I can feel them, pressing, squidging, like being attacked by firm foam.

Screw the Treaty of Versailles. Screw Clemenceau. I find a bench in a bay window and sit there with a skinny old man who hates it too. I find a way out. I discover later there is only one toilet. Not washroom, toilet. The French do this deliberately. They despise tourists. I don't blame them but the chateaux of the Loire, the Eiffel and anything else Americans like will have to do without my presence. I will only visit places other people can't stand to see. Whether this is a victory or not, I do not know.

After more than two days straight, air conditioning makes you feel ill. You are puffy inside, chilled, clearly sickening for something. You want to breathe real air, no matter how hot or polluted. This happens even when you set the air conditioner to a normal humane temperature, instead of thick-sweater temperature, as is widespread.

France wants to win back its American tourists. Only the fascists and the ninnies stayed home after France gently told Bush he was a silly, misguided man with his Iraq debacle, but whatever, Paris needs its hotels filled. So they hire Woody Allen to say in a TV ad that he doesn't want to freedom-kiss his wife but to French-kiss her. You mean, French-kiss your daughter, you respond, recoiling. How could the French think Middle America would flock to France, enormous asses and all, after seeing Allen stick his tongue in the mouth of the former Korean infant his wife adopted?

An acquaintance comes out of a washroom cubicle and chats with me as we repair our makeup. We're alike, she says confidingly. We're both a class above our husbands. A tide of intense dislike rises in me. I also feel that her announcement would have more force made somewhere other than a public toilet.

A middle-aged woman with soot black hair, a husband who's blatantly cheating on her and a laugh she has clearly been told is "tinkling" approaches me in a gaudy flowered muumuu. I'm wearing a pink suit with football player shoulders (it was the 80s is all I can say in my defence). She shrieks, "Isn't it great being a Winter?"

144. Things that are manifestly not true about marzipan

S. comes up behind me in Hediard, where I am wriggling in delight at a sales counter, and explodes. "You can't buy a kilogram of marzipan balls!"

Possible responses: "Oh, can't I?"

"Make that two kilograms."

"Just fucking watch me."

I mean, the man is astonished. First, I don't think he knows what marzipan is. And somewhere, maybe forty years ago, a number landed in his head of the weight of mashed sweetened almonds that was seemly to purchase on holiday and finally, opportunity landed.

Now I keep them by the bed and am eating a bonbon each morning with my coffee until my kilogram runs out, which "may be some time," as Captain Oates said as he politely left his Scott Expedition tent to freeze to death alone. Some balls are stained scarlet, some a buttery gold. I think I shall masticate one now. For you can't regulate your spouse's marzipan purchases. It's beyond the remit.

145. Rare things

It is very difficult to be alone in Hong Kong. Many visitors say it cannot be done. The place is so packed with humanity that you congratulate yourself for being alone in your bath. Everywhere smells of people, not necessarily an unpleasant smell but unique and sad. But on a Sunday you take the funicular and wander around the Peak. And you are completely alone in the silent woods, even as you look out over that harsh city.

The Americans, with that sense of propriety that is always at odds with the rest of the world (we'll display the corpses of enemy soldiers, but you mustn't see ours), have made it very difficult to find photographs of the Twin Towers attack that we all watched hundreds of times in the week it occurred. You have to hunt them down.

When you find them, they are gaspingly stunning. We're used to vertical catastrophes and horizontal destruction but rarely do we see them combined: a horizontal attacked with a spectacular vertical result. Thus, when you see the still photos in foreign papers or film footage in documentaries, you can't believe your eyes. One tower has been hit by one plane with the top floors incinerated and those below about to go. And yet another plane appears. It is perfectly horizontal as it approaches the pristine tower next to the smoking one. It is performing a considered deliberate self-immolating evil rape. It will pierce the tower.

What did the jumpers think as they took that final leap? Did they know this would give them only ten seconds to live? It was a singular way to die. The implacable sameness of the ugly building, the thousands of windows where people did their awful office dance for decades, and then the bodies falling as if it were a normal day of quiet desperation but they had just said "The hell with this." I am particularly touched by the people in the Windows on the World restaurant who attempted to use tablecloths as parachutes. How brave and canny. They weren't to know that the 110-storey fall was so long it would rip even their clothes off, never mind their tragic sails.

146. Suitable things

I have a circular ivy bed surrounding an ash tree like a shallow green iron pot. Ivy beds in countries with snow must be planted with Baltic Ivy. Not English Ivy. Only Baltic is tough enough. This may be why you would never vacation in a Baltic country. Lithuania, Latvia and Estonia have little to offer the serious hedonist. But their ivy is a pistol.

Being buried in Père Lachaise cemetery in Paris would be a consolation, pre-croak of course. If I could have a little stone house on top of my grave and live in this green, cobbled, mossy silence interrupted only by the puzzlement of tourists looking for "Pierre Lachaise," it wouldn't be such a bad end. Better than the charmless wasteland of a Toronto traffic island with those headstones in a reddish material that looks like the rash caused by an old but tenacious orange latex Band-Aid. I inspect the blot on my skin as I write this.

147. I sit in my comfortable room

I sit in my comfortable room in the Oberoi Hotel in Calcutta. I was hot, traumatized by traffic and almost weeping when I arrived from the airport. As soon as we reached the cool marble cleanliness of the Oberoi, I thanked the gods, my soul, whatever. Below my window, the woman in the pink sari lives with her husband and four small children in a battered hut at the edge of a piece of waste ground. Her mother-in-law sits and watches. The children play amid the dirt, stones, rusted wire. The man is rarely there. There is a standpipe with water. It is used by everyone living on the street. Her long black hair is always washed and carefully pulled back into obedience. The children are washed daily with a good soapy head-scrub and a rinse with a cup dipped in a bucket. I never hear her shout or complain. She uses a straw broom to tidy the hut and the area around it throughout the day. She does everything with care and deliberation. No one appears to be actively unhappy. They, Larkin-like, never notice me watching from the high window.

We stay for a week in this room with running water and beautiful beds in a hotel with its own electric generator for Calcutta's frequent blackouts. When I leave, I have fistfuls of rupees. I know they would change her life, help in some massive way, and I prepare to go out to the waste ground to give them to her. S. persuades me of the cruelty of this, the insult to her and to the others on the street who are no less poor, and the likelihood that the others would mob me. I keep the money. I think of her often.

My father left this city to study medicine in Glasgow, so that eventually I could turn out to be me. I am grateful. I never cease to be sorry for not giving all my cash to that woman.

148. Less often I think of a beautiful girl

Less often I think of a beautiful girl, ten years old perhaps, begging on the pavement outside the huge market in Guadalajara in 1977. She was stunning, the kind of face you could exploit the way *National Geographic* did that Afghan woman with the big eyes. But she was obviously in some kind of distress, hungry or ill. Her eyes were so dark. I push away all thoughts of her because it is too painful to remember that I didn't even give her a coin, some food, a piece of jewellery she could sell.

A well-known diplomat has told a reporter a similar story. There was a three-year-old child in Peru on the street. He wanted to get medical help for the boy but his companions didn't approve. He allowed himself to be persuaded and abandoned the child to its fate. He has never forgotten this, appears to think of it as his original sin. Although he suffered many hardships himself—he is Métis and was once violently attacked by a robber in a Cape Town hotel room, barely escaping with his life—it's the memory of the boy that does it for him. He has suffered badly from deep depression for many years.

Virginia Woolf used to ask her husband to "pull the thorn," to reassure her about whatever was tormenting her at that moment. But some thorns cannot be pulled.

149. The worst dinner of my life

The worst dinner of my life took place in Venice in the restaurant of the Hotel Saturnia where we were staying. The staff were indeed saturnine and needed a shave hourly. It was called La Caravella and its dark, almost black, wood panelling was intended to suggest a Venetian ship. To me, it immediately suggested a badly carved coffin and I knew I was in for something. Cheap flower arrangements of chrysanthemums and baby's breath and daisies dominated the room, with five looming waiters per table and a clientele composed of Germans over seventy with pork fat curling out of the corners of their mouths, and desiccated American ladies in statement hats.

I never mind prices, but I do now because I know they will be charged for very bad foods. I have a fish soup with a skinny, bony fish draped over the edges of the bowl. S. has orange Rice Krispies squares. My amaretto soufflé is a grey rice pudding. Crepes Suzette are served with a celebratory air fresh from 1952. I wait for the Zyklon B to come through the vents. We argue.

Back in the room, which has brown walls, brown furniture, brown velvet sofa, a brown bedspread and a brown headboard, I drink an entire bottle of warm white wine and write a fantastically bad ode to La Caravella:

Cabin Fever

My wood is brown; not sand, beige, taupe, suede.
Your word is bruno; no man, no sage, hope, made.
We are in the land of old.
White hair, pale flesh, bleached taste.
I am in the land of cold.
Black hair, annoyance, haste.

Soup Venetian-style—that means fish.
Soup Venetian-style—that means dish (up the client's bones)
They snap, yield nothing,
They gap, yield yap,
And a gelatinous orange liquid curves around them.

Six waiters hover; a pale white lady in red velvet is near death.
They talk of Jackie O, who had hair.
It is dark; fire, sauces, pans in coal gloom,
As if I am about to be sautéd
Not sauved.

Germans surround me. Allemandes. Cold. Harsh.
Ausgang looks good despite our fraternal world.
Odd looks are exchanged at breakfast.

As I say, I was very drunk.

150. New York

It's a big, dirty apple, I say, and not my type of city (for one thing, the shopping is tiresome and sad. There are huge quantities of goods, certainly, but they never make me say, How the hell did they think of something that clever? the way stores in Europe do). But that's not what I dislike about New York. What's truly self-destructive is the way pedestrians don't obey traffic lights. Walk on green, stop on red. If everyone did this, cars/cabs would cross the city with both speed and sang-froid. But no one does. Thus every intersection is grid-locked. Even Calcutta does better than this because people do pay attention to the uniformed man on the platform in the centre of the intersection wielding the whistle and doing his semaphore. But New Yorkers struggle through the man-made cholesterol of the city.

151. The eerie thing about travelling

The eerie thing about travelling, whether you enjoy it or not, is the way the place goes on without you when you leave for home. Hong Kong is proceeding as normal right now. Right now, people are eating eggs Benedict in the breakfast room at the Regent, the city is fresh and full of promise, the concierge is reassuring anxious tourists, the main desk is humming, the arcade doorman is attentive, the gleaming elevators are dinging away and warm water is bubbling in the waterfall pool above Victoria Harbour. Someone is in my bed. Right now. A waiter at the Café Castiglione in Paris is still there, five years after he first served us café au lait. I saw him again last week. He is aging, and gains another twenty pounds every couple of years. I think of you often, I want to say to him. I like to think that he and his family have a stable life that gives him happiness. I cannot think of any way in which my approaching him and making this remark in pidgin French would not end in a catastrophic misunderstanding. Perhaps he will think I am offering him cocaine in exchange for his passport. I'll be arrested for the corruption of waiters.

152. I visit the site of Princess Diana's death

I visit the site of Princess Diana's death as I always do when I am in Paris. I learned of her death at about 2 A.M. that night when I had insomnia and turned on CNN, which in those days was a reasonably sane news channel. We are of course reporting the death of Princess Diana, the announcer said, and I sat rigid until something broke inside me and I wept endlessly. I woke up S. who said something like Diana Who? and went back to sleep and it was either divorce him or forgive him. (We are still married.)

I still cry over her death. When I see her picture I am always taken aback, having forgotten just how beautiful she was and what love and kindness showed in her face. We knew every inch of her. There is a perfectly loving book with marvellous photographs of her that, with good intentions, still shows us a sick close-up of her tanned, perfect feet in white Chanel court shoes with black toes, a shot taken of her in Washington in June 1997. I can see the veins under her skin, the line of her big toe where it fits tightly into the shoe, the small almost invisible lines at the front of her ankle.

Do you know the only time when we know a foot that well? When it's the foot of our own child. She would not have wanted us staring at her foot after her death, knowing she would die within two months. She would not have wanted that appalling coroner to intone six years later that he had seen into her womb, and nothing was being assembled therein. She wasn't given the choice. There's no doubt I am violating human privacy in a sick modern way, just as I did when the Lyndon Johnson archives released his taped phone conversations with Jackie Kennedy. They were made a few days after Jack died. I listened online and heard that absurd breathy girlish voice say things I had never been intended to hear and felt I was raping her. What a shameful intrusion Johnson had no right to create, the archivists had no right to release and I had no right to share in.

If Diana seems little mourned now (I do not actually believe this is true; good people do not wish to be mocked for sentimentality and thus cry over her privately), it is because we have grown used to the notion of beauty and fame being unconnected to compassion. Diana united these things; there are no more Dianas. We may not have noticed it yet, but AIDS and HIV, leprosy and land mines are scarcely mentioned. The new fatalism of this century is deeply sad.

When I get to the gold flame a few hundred yards away from the spot in the tunnel where it happened, I am in floods of tears and so are other people. The first time, I left flowers not just at the ersatz memorial but at the entrance to the tunnel where you could see the last thing she saw, the Eiffel Tower lit up at night, and then the dim yellow lights of the tunnel and the thirteenth pillar. When we returned from Versailles, the tour bus took the fast route which, to my horror, went through the tunnel at the Place de l'Alma over the place where the kind French doctor, not knowing that her heart was bleeding through its rip, attempted to resuscitate her, pressing on her heart and probably hastening her death.

The florist had suggested calla lilies which she was said to have liked but they were her death flowers and I couldn't do it.

This third visit, I placed white roses that the florist twisted individually into an almost solid cone of white, protected by thick greenery. I saw this as emblematic either of imprisonment or the way she gleamed through the things that encased her. A young and extremely beautiful girl was being photographed by her mother in front of the memorial and it's a better picture than the one of me looking as though my face has been scrunched sideways by a high wind.

To the credit of the city of Paris, there is now a beautiful and well-maintained rose garden above the tunnel and carefully placed fences prevent any mourner from entering the tunnel on foot, which they must obviously have been trying to do. I felt much calmer on my third visit than on the first when the place was almost squalid.

A friend of hers said with certainty what Diana would have said of the millions of flowers that could be seen from the sky as planes landed in London. "For me?" She would have been astonished and disbelieving. She never knew how loved she was. But good people never do know that.

To this day, Diana attracts a particular venom from men and some older women. Earl Spencer saw this. "I don't think she ever understood why her genuinely good intentions were sneered at by the media, why there appeared to be a permanent quest on their behalf to bring her down. It is baffling. My own and only explanation is that genuine goodness is threatening to those at the opposite end of the moral spectrum." I now see him at that opposite end, thanks to Paul Burrell's revelations in *A Royal Duty*. But it was a thunking blow in a fight that continues.

Attitudes to Princess Diana are a handy method of dividing people into kind/not kind. I cannot like anyone who insults her memory and I do not acknowledge them.

Diana's suffering in life angers me, even as I understand that she taught us a great deal and we learned from her pain and her courage. I don't think she would have objected to this statement. She would have thought her suffering was worth it.

153. Things that are going

Novels that acknowledge no one's keyboarding and collation skills and are dedicated to one person only

Carefree airline travel now that you know it's the ozone layer's boll weevil

Bras without wire

Shake 'N Bake

Pubic hair shaved like Hitler's moustache

154. Things that are gone

Answering machines with tiny tape cassettes

School playgrounds with trees and grass

Huge department store cabinets of Butterick, Simplicity, McCall's and Vogue dress patterns displayed in catalogues and filed by code number. Bolts of cloth displayed like headstones in a ring.

New Freedom maxi-pads in purple boxes and airy-fairy dandelion things blowing in the breeze

Thermos bottles

Vinyl roofing on cars

Carpet sweepers

The Buttoneer. They were sold on TV by Ronco, I think. You sewed buttons back on with a little hand-held device. I'd kill for a Buttoneer.

155. My husband is obsessed with parking

My husband is obsessed with parking. We once attended a party at a university where parking, as at all universities, was at a premium. This was hinted at in the invitation. He dropped me off at the party and went off to park. An hour passed. I became increasingly anxious because unless he had died in a tragic parking set-to, he was going to be horrible when he arrived, just horrible. I drank more. Two hours later, he showed up in a state of rage. He had parked three miles away in a garage far off the campus. No, he did not want a glass of wine. No, he did not want a shrimp tartlet. No, he did not want to say hello to the author's mother. We're at a party,

I hissed. I whispered a suggestion. He lost his temper. No, I do not want to fucking meet David Frum. He. Said. Very. Loudly. It was so rude that even I, swaying winely, registered a change in temperature. They charge six dollars an hour at this lot, S. said with real pain. And then he left to get the car. Again. I suppose the funny part is that a man obsessed with successful parking spent the entire evening doing it badly, i.e., failing to find any. I attended a plain old party. He attended a parking soirée.

156. Different ways of speaking

The halted, stumbling manner of George W. Bush speaking without help, as though he were always anticipating saying "you fuckers, you fucking fuckers" because he knows he wants to say it but knows he must not.

The relaxed colloquial manner of George W. Bush when he is drunk at his pal's wedding. His words have an edge but that is belied by how easily they flow. The man is actually funny.

Just as Russians soften names with a "schka," Australians are lavish with nicknames. An outhouse is a "dunny." When they don't have a nickname, they shorten the noun and add a "y" or "i". Lipstick is "lippy." Football is "footy." University is "uni."

In job interviews, people bubble-speak absurdities. "Where do you see yourself five years from now?" the interviewer asks. "On another continent, moneyed and unwrinkled, loved by all who encounter me and displaying the storied torsal red flush of a recent orgasm," is what you wish to say. "With my skills honed, I'd like to be ready for the next level," is what you should say. The first would doom you in his eyes. The second would doom you in your own. So you say, "Five? I'm more worried about forty!" which is pointless, unanswerable really. If the situational math is correct, your questioner will be long dead before forty years pass.

157. Death count

When I hear that my Grade 5 teacher drowned in a boating accident while trying to rescue his companions, I start totting up the ghosts. One drowned inexplicably during a calm midnight swim, another burned to death in a "controlled burn" to fight fires in northern Ontario, one was paralyzed, another's baby crushed to death by a garage door, one killed in a KAL flight shot down by the Soviets in 1983, a friend's husband whose school friend was murdered by a cannibal in London in the early 1980s, a friend's high school friend murdered by a serial killer in the 1970s. I remember a pool of blood outside the library where a bicycle rider, the son of a judge sitting in court as it happened, had been crushed to death by a garbage truck. I recall a suicide whose remains I followed along the railroad track until it became white bits instead of red bloody bits and I agreed with the police officer that it was best not to go further. I once bought a set of black padded coat hangers in a department store from a salesclerk later convicted of a particularly cruel child murder. These are just the oddities. Cancers don't count. I read Jon McGregor's novel *If Nobody Speaks of Remarkable Things,* about a day in the life of an ordinary London street when one terrible thing takes place amid tens of thousands of other moments of interest. I feel flattened. Murder is just one more in a volume business of remarkable things that I can't track without going mad. There are billions of brain cells waiting to be stuffed with them.

158. Things that are unpleasant to see

I am wearing makeup for a TV show on which I am to babble about books, no worries there. But pre-show, my face is lacquered, my eyebrows look like crow's wings and my mouth like broken crystal with two red points. My black-lined eyes look like guns. Really, they could shoot flames, sustain powder burns. My hair has been taught such a lesson that it goes haywire for a week after just to flaunt its freedom. The young woman pulls it straight and disciplines it with a gold curling iron with a two-inch barrel, each time yowling at the pain of the heat on her hands. My head looks like a black bullet. No one gives me a second glance so all I can do is hope this is standard practice, but I have never looked less like myself. At least I assume this is so, as I would never voluntarily watch myself on television.

The elderly American tourists gather outside the tour-bus office unwisely situated on the rue de Rivoli and block the sidewalk and the bike path. Only old Americans have enough money to visit Paris for a week, apparently. The young ones must be in hostels or fleapits. A ninety-year-old man who shouldn't even be travelling is standing in the bike path. A Frenchman speeds along on his bike, knocking him to the ground. We rush to his aid. The Frenchman looks back. "Fuck you!" he yells at the old man.

An old woman berates a middle-aged salesclerk in Bloomingdale's in New York for not serving her immediately. Her stance shouts ego. Her face is contorted with rage and frustration like an evil baby's. "I have a cane!" she shouts, though whether she means to use it as a weapon or as a means of evoking pity is unclear. The ugliest part of the scene is the reaction of the saleswoman who lowers her head and shrinks her shoulders, like a dog accustomed to random beatings.

A wealthy Arab family comes to sit by the rooftop pool of the Hotel Arts in Barcelona. There are seven of them, an old couple in long robes who sit regally while their sons kit up the beach umbrella. The sons are dressed expensively in casual swimwear. There are two kids, an infant daughter who is completely ignored and a whiny little boy who is treated like a sun god. The men ignore their wives who, despite the intense heat, are dressed in pantsuits, black leather clogs, headscarves and sunglasses. Their skin is white compared to that of their husbands, a white that is not just the result of sheltering from the sun. They were chosen for their whiteness.

The grandparents are on their chairs. The men lounge on chaise longues and their wives dry them off and generally dance attendance. The wives are relegated to little plastic side tables. And the last person, a Filipina maid, squats. Worse, there is a curious intimacy between one of the men and the maid. One of the wives smiles at me shyly, but I keep thinking of the squatting servant.

It's a pool where women go topless. I have done so. Although the Germans seem comfortable with it, the British men around the pool cannot cope. But I cannot see how I could possibly tan my breasts in front of this family without arousing lust/rage/envy/contempt and, indeed, I don't wish to upset the old people. In the end, I and several other Western women loudly order about our amused husbands in order to make a point, and then depart.

159. Pleasing things

A reader emails me a picture of the baby girl she adopted from China. Her name is Sophie. Her lips look like pulpy rubies, their upper line perfectly waved like a bow. Yet she laughs like an old smoker when she's tickled, a guttural vulgar laugh, her mother says. Was she a lady from Shanghai in a previous incarnation?

The smell of L'Occitane's sweet almond soap. You feel an intense return to a place you've never been, somewhere Tennyson's lotus eaters might have lolled.

You are asked by a magazine to write fifteen hundred words about *Pride and Prejudice*. You read the novel again, watch the BBC adaptation and then write the piece in one sitting and have a splendid time. A letter comes back. We love your article! We love you! They enclose a large cheque. Money for nothing, as they say. The pleasure was all mine.

There's a laneway behind the local supermarket that you drive through to get to the main parking lot. And there is a sign saying Speed Bump. For years now, despite the best efforts of the supermarket people, the sign gets changed in the middle of the night to Pee Bum, or Pee Pump. It doesn't matter how often they repaint or floodlight or set up security cameras; for years, people have been sneaking in at 2 A.M. to satisfy a basic human need: To change a sign to Pee Bump. Tee hee. I love this. I laugh every time. It gives me faith in the human race.

Green onions grilled by accident. Exquisite. I had forty years to do this to an onion. Time wasted.

Eero Saarinen saying of his famous white moulded chairs swiveling on a single central tube, "I wanted to clear up the slum of legs."

The Museum of Medieval History in Paris has an ancient wooden carving showing small figures on parade. They are waving wooden clitorises in the air. And to think we fear mentioning them. In the Middle Ages, they were a float in the Easter Parade.

160. Outstandingly splendid things

You are in the process of writing this book. Suddenly you realize that you are not writing for a newspaper. You may make a joke, even a tasteless one, or even a bloody good one without fearing the appearance of an I Fail To See letter on the editorial page. I fail to see the humour of, they write, and it could be anything at all. You can write "fuck." You can write "My god you're stupid. Take a pill. Take several pills" as I did to one fantastically dim and ingratiating letter writer who berated me for one gentle joke in a column about depression. She responded by saying she would show my letter to everyone she knew so they would know what kind of person I was. Now that's funny. "Look, this woman I admire so much tells me I'm shockingly stupid." Wouldn't it be better to burn it? My god, she was a stupid creature.

You are on your honeymoon in London and walking idly along George Street with a huge bunch of flowers, on the way to Oddbins to pick up a bottle of wine for that night. A man passes. What a fine-looking man, you think. He calls out. And you realize it is the man you've married.

—

161. Outstandingly splendid things that give one pause

What if it hadn't been your husband you thought was so attractive that spring day in London on your honeymoon? What if you'd been alone? He broods. Decades later, he objects to me travelling alone to Paris, on the eccentric grounds that I might get drunk and accidentally sleep with a waiter. I regret the technicality of marriage that he even has a say in this. I rage and shout. But in my heart, I know it would cause hurt to that handsome man I met that day on George Street. So I love, honour and say okay, which rhymes with obey.

And a tiny part of me knows that I am one of those rare people who, after more than three glasses of wine and a Rohypnol, could trip and accidentally sleep with a waiter. I mean, it could happen. I guess.

162. *Lacrimae rerum*

Lacrimae rerum is a Latin phrase that is difficult to translate. "The tears of the world" is one suggested meaning. This is what I think now. It is true madness to end the day by watching the evening news but because of my work, I do. The pity of things, the *lacrimae rerum*. The tears of the world flow like the Yangtze.

Acknowledgments

To the women friends who have never let me down—Jennifer Allford (and her Niall and Jean); Jennifer Lanthier (and her Nicola, James and Buzz); my friend of longest standing, Rosanna Serpa, who told me never to hold back out of fear; artist Pam Davies who taught me that shapes were the crucial element; my dear Liz Clarkson, a clinical psychologist who unfortunately lives far away in Perth, Australia, but whose catchphrase "No drama" has allowed me to dismiss much aggravation over the years; Anne Kingston, who waves away the worries and orders me another glass of wine; and Lee-Anne Goodman, who strides in her seven-league boots. Much love to my girls, my string of pearls—beauteous Alexandra; Sarah the sprite; Samantha straight and tall; and Victoria, trailing clouds of glory.

My love for my gentle mother Laura has grown over the years as I realized the extent of her courage and endurance. To my sister Hazel, it is a truth universally acknowledged that she is the nice one.

Thanks to my agent Denise Bukowski and her associate Jackie Joiner (containing Amelia) for being on my side, Michael Schellenberg for feeding me cake, Penguin editorial director Diane Turbide, who is queen of all she surveys, copy editor Karen Alliston for laughing in the right places, Penguin senior designer Cathy MacLean for her instant understanding, the wonderful Tracy Bordian and Lesley Horlick, who nursed the baby, and David Davidar, Canada's king Penguin, for not losing patience with this non-fiction creature. And gratitude forever to my pit crew, the musicians Jann Arden, Steve Earle, Annie Lennox, Sarah McLachlan, Joni Mitchell, Blue Rodeo, Carly Simon, "Little Wing," Rickie Lee Jones and Bob Marley. Special gratitude to Gianfranco Bortolato, playing Albinoni's Adagio on the oboe with the Interpreti Veneziani in Venice's San Bartolomeo church, who taught me to lift up mine eyes.

And thank you to the writers who cover pain with jokes, which is by far the best way—Lewis Black, Helen Fielding, Stephen Fry, Phil Hogan, Jean Kerr, Rick Mercer, Mil Millington, John O'Farrell, David Sedaris, Mark Steel and Mary Walsh.